ALI'S
BOOK OF
TALL
TALES

Random thoughts
from the 2nd row

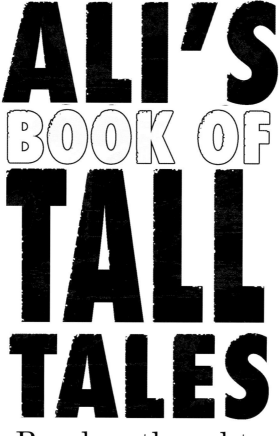

ALI'S BOOK OF TALL TALES

Random thoughts from the 2nd row

with James Griffin

Hodder Moa

National Library of New Zealand Cataloguing-in-Publication Data
Williams, Ali, 1981-
Ali's book of tall tales : random thoughts from the 2nd row /
Ali Williams with James Griffin.
ISBN 978-1-86971-156-6
1. Williams, Ali, 1981-. 2. Rugby union football players—
New Zealand—Biography. 3. Rugby union football—New Zealand.
I. Griffin, James. II. Title.
796.333092—dc 22

A Hodder Moa Book
Published in 2009 by Hachette New Zealand Ltd
4 Whetu Place, Mairangi Bay
Auckland, New Zealand
www.hachette.co.nz

Designed and produced by Hachette New Zealand Ltd
Printed by 1010 Printing International Ltd., China

The publishers wish to acknowledge the assistance of Greg Dyer, of Essentially Group, in the
publication of this book.

Ali would like to thank all his rugby mates and his non-rugby mates too.

James would like to thank Kate for the hook-up; Warren and Kevin for the patience and fine wine; and Tanz, Ruby and Max for everything else.

CONTENTS

A WORD OF WARNING ABOUT THIS BOOK

Some of the stories in this book are the result of drinking alcoholic beverages. Sometimes they're the result of drinking too many alcoholic beverages. But they are in no way meant to promote the drinking of alcoholic beverages or to glorify the boozy, binge-drinking culture we have in this country. They are simply telling it like it is; which is that when you're a professional sportsman, sometimes you need to cut loose.

You don't get that many opportunities to cut loose, these days — what with the number of games you play across a season, and the way you need to look after yourself, as an athlete, if you want to make it through those games. The days of the court session after every game are very much a thing of the past now.

But guys need to be guys; and when you're young (or relatively young), fit and playing for the best footie team on the planet, you need to be able to enjoy those things — and from time to time that involves cutting loose. That's just a fact of life; that's the way it is. And that's sometimes where the best yarns are found — in the way things can go from bad to worse and then spin totally out of control after a few quiet ones.

And, to be totally honest, a book full of stories of the boring stuff I do 90 per cent of the time — training, sleeping, business stuff, hanging round the house doing not very much — hell, who'd want to read about all that stuff?

Except maybe the sleeping bit. That's good, sleeping. There's a chapter in here on sleeping because most of the time that's as exciting as it gets for me, because that's how Ali Williams rolls.

You have been warned is all I'm saying here.

HERE IS SOME BASIC STUFF YOU SHOULD KNOW ABOUT BEFORE YOU START READING THIS BOOK

Okay, I suppose, if you want to be 100 per cent accurate, you already started reading the book when you read the bit that said A WORD OF WARNING ABOUT THIS BOOK, but let's just call that the warm-up and say you've started reading it now, and that there's some stuff you need to know before you go too much further.

Do not take anything in this book too seriously. That's really important here. This is not to say that we all didn't take it seriously when we put the book together or that there isn't some serious stuff in here, because there is. In fact, a lot of the stuff that is kinda serious in this book is about the trouble that started

'Seriously, I once caught a fish about yay big. No bullshit.'

with me opening my mouth and then people taking seriously whatever came out of it. All I'm saying is you shouldn't take this book too seriously because, generally, in my opinion, it's when people take me seriously that the trouble starts. I hope that makes everything clear.

This book isn't in any actual order so you don't need to start at the beginning and read all the way through to the end. Unless you want to, of course; if that is what works for you, sweet, because I'm just pointing out that you can dip in and out of it, whenever and at whatever page you like, without worrying that you'll lose the plot. Some people reckon I lost the plot years ago, so maybe that's why this book is the way it is.

There are some rude words in this book. If that offends you, skip over them and pretend they're not there. Also you're probably reading the wrong book, because this is a book by a rugby player and rugby isn't about tea and cucumber sandwiches (except maybe in some of the more posh parts of England). Rugby players aren't, as a bunch, backward in coming forward with the odd expletive from time to time. Man up and deal with the odd spot of swearing.

Not that this book is all about rugby. It's mainly about rugby because that's what I do, but there's lots of other stuff in here as well because I live in the same world as everyone else — well, almost — and I have thoughts about things that aren't to do with rugby, so we wrote some of them down as well, just because we could.

I'm only pointing this out in case some boof-head reading this book goes 'Hang on, what the hell has this got to do with rugby?' and gets all bent out of shape about it. Just warning you, okay, so there are no unpleasant surprises further on down the track.

If you're reading in the toilet — which is cool, 'cause the dunny is as good a place as any to read, especially if you're a bloke — please don't be tempted, even in an emergency, to use the pages of this book for any purpose other than what they're meant for. Anything other than actual reading of the pages is just disrespectful to all the people who put a lot of time and effort into this book.

Also, if you're reading in the bog, don't forget to wash afterwards because that's good hygiene.

Wash your hands, that is, not the book 'cause washing the book will make the pages go all soggy and then stick together when it dries out.

And if you're doing anything else that might make the pages of this book stick together, that's just wrong and I don't want to know. Get help if that's what you're into.

Above all, remember that everything you read within these pages may or may not be true. And don't expect any clues as to which is which, because in the end it doesn't really matter. This is a collection of thoughts and experiences and stuff that cracked me up at the time and, yes, stuff that pissed me off at the time. You guys can figure out what's what as you go along.

As long as, remember, you don't take anything in these pages too seriously. Keep that in mind and we'll get along just fine.

MARIAH CAREY AND ME
The truth behind the rumours

This is 2002 and it's my first tour with the ABs. We're in Paris, chilling out for a bit. I'm sitting in the lobby of the hotel, with Doug Howlett and Christian Cullen, and we're keen to do something but not entirely sure what.

The answer rolled into the room in the form of Jonah, who was taking Tana off to this party he knew of. Only Jonah would know of a party in Paris. Maybe he was taking pity on us, but he says we can tag along and off we go — me and the rock stars — into a November Paris night.

We end up walking down the Champs-Élysées until, up ahead, there's this crowd outside this club. Not a small crowd either, I mean we're talking in the hundreds here. And we get to the outskirts of the crowd, and I'm scoping things out, wondering who the hell is inside, when these bouncers start cutting through the crowd towards us. And these bouncers are monsters,

Me and Jonah showing Steve Devine what the world looks like from our height.

bigger than Jonah, and suddenly they're surrounding us.

Well, actually they're all surrounding Jonah, saying 'Jonah Lomu! Jonah Lomu!' And they start herding him towards the door. So I make sure I'm in the circle as we're cutting through the crowd toward the club. 'Jonah Lomu! Jonah Lomu!' I wish I could say I heard someone gasp 'and Ali Williams too!' but that would be a lie too big even for this book.

Inside the club and Jonah (and his entourage consisting of the rest of us) are taken straight to the VIP section, sat down and given beers. And then Jonah gets whisked off to have his photo taken and do the Jonah-thing that Jonah does better than anyone else. Meanwhile we sit there, drinking our beers, spotting the famous people (who the other guys knew and I didn't have a clue) and generally feeling pretty cool.

But the thing about VIP areas is that they're cooler as an idea, from the outside, than when you're in them; with everyone on the outside looking at you like you think you're someone special just because you're in the VIP area. It's like you're in an aquarium and all the people looking in at the fish think the fish are totally up themselves. This is why, after a few beers, me, Tana, Doug and Christian are over this, and we're ready to go find some normal people and drink beer with them.

As we're getting up to leave, I see across the club, also getting ready to leave, with her own set of bouncers, Mariah Carey. And she's looking across at me. And then she waves at me.

18

Holy shit, I'm thinking, Mariah Carey is waving at me.

So I wave back.

Then I realise Tana, Doug and Christian are also waving at Mariah Carey. Clearly they also think Mariah Carey is waving at them.

And then we all realise; and we all turn round . . .

And there is Jonah, waving back to Mariah Carey, who is clearly waving to him because, well, he's Jonah and the rest of us mere mortals aren't.

There's still a tiny part of me that wonders, to this day, if Mariah ever thinks back to that night, in the club, in Paris, and wonders who the big goose was with Jonah, the one who waved at her.

I suspect not.

Mariah Carey: she still wants me.

WORLD FAMOUS
IN NEW ZEALAND

I know it's an occupational hazard, and I'm not whining about it because I wouldn't change what I do for the world, but it can still be freaking weird, being in the public eye all the time, here in New Zealand. It's like people claim to know you, because in some respect — the stuff they see on TV or read in the papers or whatever — they do kinda know you, a tiny bit of you. And then some of the ones who actually do get to know you, even for just a minute or two, they *really* want to know you.

Like I went into this bakery, a while ago, to get a sandwich, and there's this bloke in there — a supplier or something — talking to the people behind the counter. He was South African, as it turned out — not that it really matters — and he sees me and clocks who I am and figures it's cool to start up a conversation, about playing rugby, or not playing rugby because I was injured at the time. And I politely answer his questions, have a bit of a yarn, play the game the way it's meant to be played.

But things start going on a bit so, me being me, I can't help but think 'I'll just be a cheeky prick here'; so I start taking the piss, turning it back on him. And I start asking him about his rugby career — when he'll be back from injury and all that kind of stuff. And bugger me if he doesn't start going off, launching into this whole story about how he did his knee in and so forth. And on he goes, telling anyone who'll listen — which is me and the shop-owners — all about everything; going on like he's known me for years and we're best mates.

And I'm standing there, smiling, thinking, 'Shit, all I came in for was a sandwich.'

Yet another example of me needing to learn not to open my big mouth, I suppose.

But, in the end, for me it's about being comfortable — finding that place where you're comfortable being you. That's why when you're in the boat I'm in, you feel most comfortable with your rugby mates — or, come to think of it, actually out in a boat, on the water, far away from everything.

But back on dry land, I tend to hang with the rugby boys, the ones who are basically in the same position as me. They know that your actions have a consequence — good or bad. And that extends even to the level where some kid who wants an autograph is either going to walk away thinking you're a good bloke or a jerk, depending on how you deal with it. And how you deal with it depends on a lot of things — like how you're feeling at the time, whether they've caught you at a really bad moment or not.

Not that you can go round thinking like that, every single moment, otherwise you'll just burn yourself up, beat yourself up over every little thing. I should be able to look back on my time as an All Black without going 'Shit, if only I'd enjoyed my position a bit more.' So I do. I enjoy myself and there's nothing wrong with that.

And then I end up in the gossip papers because I happen to run nude down Ponsonby Road. It all ends up in the papers, but shit, who really cares? Be yourself; be true to what you are.

Me, trying to remember how to spell my name. A . . . L . . . umm . . .

BEST COACH I'VE EVER PLAYED UNDER?

Peter Barton. Kings College 1st XI cricket coach, even though he once sent me from the field for arguing with an umpire.

SLEEP
MY VERY
SCIENTIFIC STUDY

Based on my extensive investigations, over a fair old period of time now, by studying the sleep patterns of my many and varied team-mates over my career, I can now conclude that in terms of ability to sleep for long periods of time, the top five ethnic sleeping groups in the world are:

1st — Fijians
2nd — Croatians
3rd — Samoans
4th — Tongans
5th — Kiwis

Having come to these conclusions I would like to add that, as a Kiwi, I sleep well above the national average; certainly up there with the Croatians.

THE JOY OF SLEEP

I love sleep. I'm not afraid to admit this publicly; in fact, I will stand bollock naked on the terraces at Eden Park to declare my love of sleep to the world. Not that I'm planning to actually do that, mind you — I'm just making the point here that there is nothing wrong with liking to sleep as much as humanly possible; and then some.

They reckon that the average human being needs between seven and nine hours of sleep a day to be on top of their game when they're awake. Now, I reckon because I'm slightly larger than the average human being, I actually need a lot more than this, just to function properly.

We used to have a pet rabbit once; it had this disease called Flopsy or Rabbit Sleeping Sickness or some such thing — I never really have been good at remembering details like that. Actually, I think Flopsy was a character in a book, come to think of it. None of which is really of any importance because the point I'm getting to is that whatever the disease our rabbit had, it was apparently caused by inbreeding (it was from West Auckland; apparently they get a lot of that stuff out there), and it meant that every now and then it would just fall asleep.

Awake one second, zonked out the next, lying on the floor not moving — the first time it happened we thought it was dead. And when I say 'asleep' I mean 'completely coma'd out'. And it would stay coma'd out for days on end.

We used to have to feed it through a straw down its throat, just to keep it alive while it was asleep. Then, after a few days, for no reason you could figure out, it'd be up on its feet again like nothing untoward had happened. Freaky shit.

But on the other hand, apart from the inbreeding stuff and the bit where you have a straw jammed down your throat, I couldn't help but think that if ever I get some kind of freaky disease, that something along the lines of the freaky rabbit sleeping disease would be the one for me. Just to be able to fall asleep wherever I like (and trust me, I can sleep anywhere — cars, buses, aeroplanes, you name it, I'm snoozing) and for as long as I like. Bliss, mate.

In fact, to go one step better, if I could organise it so that the disease kicked in only when I'm lying on the couch, in front of the TV, that would be perfection; because as anyone who loves sleep as much as me will tell you, there is something truly special about falling asleep in front of the TV. Maybe it's the voices or the car chases or the gunfire coming from the TV that lull you into falling asleep, and then feed messages straight into your subconscious; into your dreams.

Whatever it is, as a master of sleep, I can heartily recommend couch/TV sleeping as the way to go.

As an illustration of how much I love sleep — and, very importantly, how the love of sleep should never be confused with laziness — let me take you through how an ideal game day, with an evening kick-off, pans out for me, starting when the clock ticks over to 1 minute after midnight, of that day:

12.01am to 9am: sleep.

9am-ish to 10am: breakfast at the hotel; talk to people, go back to room for . . .

10am to 11.30am-ish: more sleep.

11.30am-ish to 12pm-ish: loll around in hotel room, realising there is no time left for sleep because it is almost time for . . .

12pm-ish to 1.30pm-ish: lunch at hotel, chew the fat with the boys while chewing the food; important team-bonding time.

1.30pm-ish to 2pm: bus to venue for captain's run; ideally catch a bit of a snooze on the way.

2pm to 2.45pm-ish: captain's run, practise lineouts and so forth; no chance for sleeping here.

2.45pm-ish to 3pm-ish: bus back to hotel; snoozing less likely now.

3pm-ish to 4pm-ish: pick up jersey from manager's room (if match day is a test match); have last feed before match; no sleeping possible during all this.

4pm-ish to 5pm-ish: time for one last sleep before the game, just to make sure body and mind are raring to go.

5pm-ish to kick-off time: opportunities for sleep long gone now in flurry of activity — medical staff strapping various parts of the body that need to be strapped; team meeting; watching Geoff Thomas's fishing show on TV if game day is on a Saturday in New Zealand on a day when it is on; get gear sorted; get onto bus and go to venue; get dressed for game; chew fingernails and get psyched up; run onto pitch.

As you'll see from all that, sleep is an important part of being a professional athlete today — or at least it is for this particular professional athlete. And if anyone out there takes what I'm saying here as further proof that the All Blacks of today have gone soft, let me put to you this question: would you prefer to smash Schalk Burger in a head-on, one-on-one tackle, when you're both running at each other full-tit, *after* you've had an adequate amount of sleep; or *without* an adequate amount of sleep?

Sure, I know that life is very much a case of 'to each their own' but, just quietly, I definitely know the answer I'd pick.

And, on that note, I'm going to lie in front of the telly for a bit.

STRONGEST PLAYER, POUND-FOR-POUND?

If I don't say Brad Thorn I will get in trouble.

MOST NATURALLY GIFTED PLAYER?

My brother.

THE HAKA AND ME

I know this probably isn't the wisest thing to say out loud, but once upon a time I was never into the haka. Sure, like just about every other New Zealander I was totally aware of its importance, not only to the All Black tradition, but to the country as a whole, but I still couldn't buy into it; not because I'm not Maori, but because I got so nervous doing it. I just really, really didn't want to stuff it up in front of everyone.

So for a while there I'll cop to pretty much going through the motions when it came to the haka. Get out there, get it done, get into the game; that was me. That was what the haka meant to me, another thing to be ticked off before we got into the main event.

Then we had this guy come in, Derek Lardelli, who talked to the boys and from the ground up — literally — he taught us what the haka really means. And Derek was awesome. And he changed the whole way I looked at it.

I remember Derek telling us how you get out of the haka what you *want* to get out of it; not what you *think* you should get out of it. I guess it might sound selfish saying this, but as a professional athlete, taking this pre-match ritual and learning how it could go from being something we had to do, to something that could truly help me get through the next 80 minutes, that changed my mind-set like you wouldn't believe.

Derek talked to us about how the haka is actually about bringing your ancestors out from the ground, stuff along those lines, to help you face the challenge in front of you and your team-mates — which is obviously the blokes standing across from you. It's getting you physically ready for battle, as well as getting you psyched up for battle.

It's about saying we are a team, ready to take anything you throw at us and give it back, with interest.

Okay, now even I could understand that. I'm hearing that and thinking 'Yeah, that works, that works for me.' So I started to embrace the whole haka idea; I got how I could respect the tradition and the culture and, to cut a long story short, get over myself.

But understanding the haka; and then performing the haka in front of 40,000 people and God knows how many people watching on the TV — these are two very different things. So I decided that no way would I end up standing in the middle of the group because that's where the cameras used to focus while we're doing the haka. And I was (and still am, just for the record) completely happy with letting the guys who know what they're doing, haka-wise, be the ones who represent it on the screens of the nation.

This is why I moved out to the side of the guys, when we're doing the haka. In the front, but way out the side, so I could be this big goober on the wing, doing his thing and not getting in the way of the dudes who know what they're doing. And once I was there and I was happy and I knew the meaning behind it, I started getting into it, big time, and adding my own touches to the haka — sticking the tongue out and advancing towards the opposition and stuff like that.

Now, of course, they've got cameras everywhere, covering everything, so there's nowhere for me to hide. But that doesn't mean I'm going to back off because now I'm totally into it. I have completely bought into what this means, so I go into a shell and I'm focusing on what I need to do and what the team needs to do. So I end up being on camera more than I would like, because I'm this white guy who can't dance, tongue hanging out, giving the other team the stink-eye across the halfway line. I think it's fair to say I'm in a certain state when it comes to the haka.

In fact, there is a certain school of thought that wishes Williams wouldn't get so bloody wound up in the haka now because it tends to send him a bit mental for the first few minutes of the game. But we don't want to dwell on that here and now.

So does the haka give the All Blacks an unfair advantage, like various overseas media trundle out from time to time? No, of course not; it's all about the success of the All Blacks and teams looking to find a point of difference — *any* point of difference — that explains that success. Hell, in my case, like I just said, it's a complete disadvantage because I'm still amped from the haka when the kick-off comes, which isn't exactly having your head entirely in the game from the get-go.

Look, if the haka is such a problem for other teams I reckon they're more than welcome to do whatever they want in return. Sing a song; do a dance if you want; it doesn't matter. Actually the English forward pack doing an impromptu Morris dance; or the Irish giving it a bit of Riverdance; or the Scots giving us the old *Braveheart* free-willy, up with the kilts, en masse brown-eye, would be great. And great television, I'm sure — all those pasty Scottish arses in a row.

At the end of the day, at the beginning of the game, we don't really care what the opposition does when it comes to the haka. If you want to turn your back on it; that's your call, fair enough, good on you and we'll take note of that when we start the game. If you want to get the crowd to follow the haka by singing a song about some bloke who chases a sheep into a pond and drowns (and they make jokes about New Zealanders and sheep?) then that is totally up to you. If you make us perform the haka in the dressing room before the game, we'll do it, because in the end it's not about what you want; it's about what we need to do as a team. And thanks for the extra motivation, by the way.

I think, of all the ways of dealing with the haka that have been tried in the past, the Welsh have got closest to the spirit of the thing. Short of throwing leeks at us while we were mid-performance, the stand-off at the Millennium Stadium during the end-of-year tour in 2008 was great.

They didn't back down; we didn't back down.

Except for Richie, who automatically turned away at the end of the haka, to get on with the game, before he realised that no other bugger was moving and he had to come back to join the stare-down.

I detected the hand of Warren Gatland there, knowing that the basic rule of the haka is that you stink-eye the guy lined up opposite you until they accept the challenge by walking away — and if they

Picking your nose is not really a recommended way of dealing with the haka . . . and what's going on with the shorts of the bloke on the left?

don't walk away, you don't move. And so it went on and on and on and on and on. But in the end it was kind of funny, as Jonathan Kaplan and his assistants were trying to figure out a way to get these boof-heads to stop this nonsense and get the game started before the TV people got antsy.

But when all this is said and done, if you think you can crack the All Blacks by cracking them in the haka; it just doesn't work that way.

It's our tradition, so please respect it — and keep in mind it is actually the next 80 minutes that counts, not some guy with his tongue out giving it heaps and getting into your face. Just a word to the wise there.

SOME
GREAT ADVICE
FROM A GREAT MAN

I don't remember how the words went exactly, because remembering stuff exactly isn't my strong point, but apparently the nuggety piece of advice Brian Lochore gave me before the Lions series back in 2005 went something along the lines of:

'Williams, if I see you running round the place with your head in the air looking for an easy try, I'll hit you over the head with a bloody four-by-two.'

Crikey, how the hell am I going to fix this kid?

Sir Brian Lochore: a very wise man.

Scoring against the Lions: sorry Rodders, this one's all mine.

Now that's old school coaching at its genius best. And I'll tell you for nothing that it bloody well worked.

Interestingly, mind you and come to think of it, I not only played some of my best rugby in an All Black shirt against the Lions, but I also grabbed two test tries, more than I've scored against any other team.

I sometimes wonder if Brian (who, incidentally, only ever scored one try against the Lions, not that I'm rubbing it in) is out there somewhere, with his four-by-two, waiting to clobber me for those two tries.

RUGBY IS A KICKING GAME
and forwards can kick too

When you watch a test match on TV or from the stands there will usually come a time when the unthinkable will happen: a forward will kick the ball. You can almost hear the buttocks clenching, all over the nation, when some great ox has a brain explosion and decides to put his foot to it. The TV commentators suddenly get all squeaky on it in a 'what the hell does he think he's doing?' way; and then everyone holds their breath, wondering what disaster will inevitably follow.

You'd think given the way the game has changed over the years that the sight of a forward kicking the rugby ball wouldn't give everyone heart palpitations. Didn't Zinzan Brooke popping over those drop kicks, cool as you like, from out near the halfway line, against England and South Africa teach anyone that forwards can kick too? Clearly not.

Now maybe it's because I used to be a soccer player, but the idea of kicking the ball doesn't faze me at all. I know my role in the team is primarily *not* to kick — and that kicking the snot out of the ball is, for the most part, the domain of the flash boys out the back like Dan and company — but if I get the pill in a situation where kicking seems like the right option, then I'll kick the bloody thing. If I've had a chance to assess the defensive line; to look where my guys are; to see a gap downfield where we might be able to force a turnover on their lineout, then I'm going to give it a lash.

Sure, it may not work out quite as planned all the time, but that's all part of the game and it's not going to stop me doing it again. But neither should it be treated like it's some kind of minor miracle when it does come off.

> I'm a professional athlete;
> I practise this stuff; it doesn't
> just happen by accident,
> you know.

And when you look at it, the Laws of Physics are on my side when it comes to kicking the football. I'm a tall rooster, with legs in proportion to the rest of my body, which means they're longer than your average legs. This means that when I swing my boot at a rugby ball, by the time I connect with said rugby ball, I'm generating a heck of a lot of power. I'm sure there's some physics egghead out there who can figure out exactly how much power, but I bet it is way more power than, say, Dan Carter can generate with his much

Proving once and for all that I can kick a rugby ball with one hand tied behind my back.

shorter legs. Sure Dan more than makes up for this with practice, technique and brilliance, but you shouldn't automatically rule me out just because I'm a forward is all I'm saying.

And it's not just distance I can generate when I decide to put boot to ball. There's also a fair bit of finesse in these feet of mine, let me tell you. Well, in my right foot, to be completely honest, because my left is pretty much there for standing on while the other one is busy doing the actual kicking business. And as a thing of beauty to admire, of course.

As proof of this I offer up probably one of the most brilliant All Black tries ever scored; one that was all down to my deft kicking. Sure, this try isn't generally mentioned in the same breath as Jonah walking all over Mike Catt, when people gather over a few quiet ales to debate the Greatest All Black Tries of All Time, but I feel this is an oversight that will be corrected with the passing of time — and the consumption of the right number of quiet ales.

Eden Park, early September 2005, New Zealand versus Australia. If we win, we take back the Tri-Nations crown which we had lost to South Africa the previous season. (I mention this only to put the importance of this try in perspective, for when it is being discussed as potentially one of The Greatest All Black Tries of All Time, not to glorify myself in any way.) It's 20 minutes into the game and we're leading 8–0 after Leon had banged over a penalty and Richie had scored. (I mention this only to point out that it was early in the game, with the scores still close, so it wasn't one of those show-boat tries you get at the end of the game when the scoreboard's blown out, not to glorify myself in any way.) We're hot on attack and the referee has pinged them for offside, right in front of the posts. A gift three points.

The ball has ended up in the in-goal area, where Chris Jack retrieves it and flings it back to me, standing on the mark. Except I'm not standing on the mark enough for Chris White, the referee, which not only stops the possibility of a tap and go for the line, but it also gives me the chance to take a quick look around to see what's on offer.

And there, out on the right wing, all alone, is Doug Howlett, waving at me.

And I mean he's waving at me relentlessly; in a way that is very difficult to ignore. For an instant I think about taking the tap and flinging a pass out there, but really the chances of that leaking God knows where — forward, backward, over the sideline, into Australian hands — were huge. Even I'm not such a goose to give that kind of low-percentage play a shot. And Doug is still waving at me. Waving, waving . . .

So I take the tap and I delicately chip the ball in Doug's direction.

And all around me I can hear the sound of buttocks clenching, as the ball floats through the air. And I realise that the act of giving up a gift three points, to take us to 11–0, in favour of trying to kick

'Oh shit, this could go very, very wrong . . .'

To think I put my career on the line to kick the ball to this show pony.

the ball to Doug, is one of those moments where you can go from Hero to Zero real quick. If this ball ends up in the stands and we lose the game by three points or less, tomorrow's headlines will all be about how Williams' brain-snap cost us the Tri-Nations.

Of course nothing of the sort happened. With pinpoint accuracy the ball sailed out to Doug and all he had to do was catch the thing, fall over and claim the five points. But not the glory, I would argue. Expect, as Monty Python says, the unexpected.

This is not to say Ali Williams is all about the kicking game. Far from it, for there are certain facets of the kicking game I'm happy to leave to the experts — and Zinzan Brooke — as my one and only attempt at a drop kick will testify.

It was against Canterbury, back in, I think, 2002. For some reason I found myself in the pocket, out in front, with the ball in hand and a bit of time to think about things (never a good idea, that thinking about things, in my opinion).

I wasn't a huge runner of the ball, back in those days, so I ended up thinking, 'Oh well, might as well plop one over, get the three points.'

The problem was, I reckon, the thinking time + the time to get the ball from hand to ground to foot + getting the rhythm right, all added up to way too much time, so the kick got charged down — by Greg Somerville, definitely not the quickest bloke on the rugby field that day.

But not only was my first drop kick in top-flight rugby charged down by a prop, the ball was turned over and hacked down the field, with me and everyone else haring after it. It was only the fact that Sam Broomhall, I think, knocked on with the line wide open that saved my three-pointer turning into five at the other end. As we formed up for the scrum, I received some fairly stern advice from my team-mates never to try that again. So I never have.

Mind you, this isn't to say that maybe one day I won't find myself in the pocket again, with the ball in hand and a bit of time to think about things; and maybe I'll end up thinking, 'Well, three points would be good here . . .'

And who knows where that might lead?

MEMO TO SELF

In the run-up to the 2003 Rugby World Cup –
broke bone in foot.
In the run-up to the 2007 Rugby World Cup –
broke jaw.

Must try harder
not to break bits of
me in Rugby World
Cup years.

A THING YOU PROBABLY PROBABLY SHOULDN'T DO ON PONSONBY ROAD

'And then one thing led to another . . .'
That's pretty much the story of my life, right there in those seven words. Along with 'it seemed like a good idea at the time'. When I look back at a lot of the strife I've got into, over the years, those two phrases pretty much sum up a lot of it. This story is no exception.

Auckland's Ponsonby Road has a bit of a reputation; lots of bars and restaurants, lots of people out shopping during the day or having a good time at night. A busy little part of Auckland, for sure, especially round, say, 9 o'clock at night, towards the end of a working week.

So Ponsonby Road is possibly not the best place in the world to spontaneously decide to get naked and go for a bit of a run, but one

Fashion Week: clothes on.

thing had led to another and it seemed like a good idea at the time. Now there's a surprise.

Just to back it up a bit, to set the story straight, it was Fashion Week in Auckland. That doesn't mean I was trying to promote nudity as a fashion trend — that's much more Marc Ellis territory than mine. What it does mean is that for the duration of Fashion Week we'd had a couple of models, a model couple from Australia in fact — let's call them Ken and Barbie — crashing at our house. They were really good sorts, in an insanely good-looking model kind of way.

So all week Ken and I had been rarking each other up about causing some sort of scandal at Fashion Week, just to liven the thing up. The possibility of getting naked and causing a stir had been mentioned along the way, but nothing had come of it — thus far.

As an aside, and at the risk of sounding like a total Aucklander, I've got a lot of respect for a lot of what goes on at Fashion Week. Once you get past the posing and the bullshit over who gets to sit in the front row and have their picture taken, Fashion Week is largely about a bunch of people — some of whom I call my mates — trying to make a living out of something they've created. Business is business and it's tough out there no matter what you're selling so all power to them, I say. And, for the record, I like sitting in the front row because there's more leg room; and sometimes you really just don't want your picture taken, okay?

Anyway, back to the story, and this particular Fashion Week was coming to a close and still no scandal had eventuated, as Ken and I and various unnamed others of a devious and seriously delinquent nature were out for a quiet stroll down Ponsonby Road, of a night, possibly visiting the occasional beverage house, as is the way life rolls on Ponsonby Road.

It was on this stroll that the delinquent others strolling with us happened to remind Ken and me of our threat to get naked during Fashion Week. Now this sounded a lot like a dare to me and I have never been one to walk away from a dare; not even on Ponsonby Road, at night.

So off came the clothes. There was nothing else for it. Pride was at stake. Also it was a celebration of Marc's National Nude Day — only just not actually on National Nude Day. As the unnamed others gathered up the clothes in our wake, Ken and I took off, hell for leather, down Ponsonby Road, towards home.

I did actually take a bit of a detour, I must confess, through

Fashion Week: clothes still on.

the drive-through at KFC Ponsonby. It seemed like the thing to do at the time. But when I tried to order at the window the guy didn't even take my order; either he was too freaked out by this nude 2-metre-tall monster raving at him or he figured out that I probably didn't have any money to pay for it, being nude and all.

The end result was I was forced to bolt for home without any chicken.

I'm not saying this should be a regular occurrence on Ponsonby Road — nude blokes trying to get takeaway food and scaring the nice people in the restaurants — but there's nothing wrong with a bit of a celebration of the human spirit from time to time.

And anyone who says they arrived home, carrying my clothes, to find me doing stretches because I'd injured myself in the process is lying. I had a dodgy ankle that year and running barefoot — bare everything — down a Ponsonby Road footpath probably wasn't a genius move.

But it seemed like a good idea at the time.

BEST PLAYERS I'VE EVER PLAYED AGAINST?

The All Blacks, at contact training.

50

LOOK
OVER THERE!

Okay, this might not be what you'd call very politically correct, but I think blaming others in the heat of the moment can be a great way to go.

That is to say that when it all turns to custard in a horrendous fashion, and you happen to be at the centre of things, then go ahead, point the finger at whoever is closest and make it known, as loudly as possible, that it is all their fault. If, for example, you're trying to dock your boat, with a crowd watching, and it gets monumentally cocked up, make sure the crowd knows it is the fault of every other bugger on the boat except you.

Sure, in the long run, evidence might emerge to the contrary and there might have to be a reallocation of blame, but that has nothing to do with what is going on there and then. And what is going on there and then is making sure you're not the one every other bugger is pointing the finger at. Try it. Sometimes it even works.

WHO SAYS I'M INJURY PRONE?

1. INJURY: Broken jaw
    CAUSE: French caveman
    PAIN LEVEL: Not being able to talk was the biggest pain
                     – for me, at least
    RESULT: Eight weeks sucking through a straw,
                     which sucked big time

2. INJURY: Broken navicular bone in foot
    CAUSE: During running fitness test
    PAIN LEVEL: Not too bad
    RESULT: Failed fitness test, obviously; sidelined for
                     lead-up to '03 World Cup; got to model
                     my moon-boot as a fashion accessory

The jaw-breaking moment: Carl Hayman in background, making a pathetic attempt to catch me.

54

3. INJURY: Stuffed ankle
   CAUSE: Playing silly buggers
   PAIN LEVEL: Average, but didn't go away quickly
   RESULT: Had to take many pills to tough it out to keep playing

4. INJURY: Blown AC joint in shoulder
   CAUSE: When nude touch rugby goes very wrong
   PAIN LEVEL: Like a hangover; bollocking from Steve Hansen worse
   RESULT: Missed one test; humiliation

5. INJURY: Floppy finger
   CAUSE: Got finger stuck in opposition's shorts (not on purpose)
   PAIN LEVEL: Nothing to write home about
   RESULT: Finger in plastic cast for 12 weeks

6. INJURY: Back
   CAUSE: Pulling anchor up on boat – or 'doing weights' as it's officially called
   PAIN LEVEL: I'm tough; I can roll with these things
   RESULT: Couldn't move for three days; didn't play for three weeks

7. INJURY: Knee cartilage
   CAUSE: Shit happens when you run around a lot
   PAIN LEVEL: Still bloody hurts, never gets any better
   RESULT: You just play on, don't you?

8. INJURY: Getting smacked in the head
    CAUSE: Getting smacked in the head
    PAIN LEVEL: Can't remember
    RESULT: Can't remember

9. INJURY: Split head
    CAUSE: Brother hit me with hammer because I
                   caught a fish and he didn't
    PAIN LEVEL: Like I had been dropped on my head from
                   a great height
    RESULT: Blood pissing everywhere

10. INJURY: Teeth through lips
    CAUSE: Jumping over aeroplane seats until
                   suddenly there were no seats left, only wall
    PAIN LEVEL: Made worse because there were still six
                   hours to go on the flight
    RESULT: Modelling career stuffed

11. INJURY: Achilles' tendon
    CAUSE: Advancing old age
    PAIN LEVEL: Never went away, like climbing a never-
                   ending brick wall of pain
    RESULT: 2009 a complete write-off as far as playing
                   rugby went; not happy

HOW TO REMEMBER SOMEONE'S NAME

There are heaps of people on Earth. Heaps and heaps. Which means there are a lot of names to remember.

Not that you're going to meet everyone on the planet, of course. That'd take way too long and you'd never get anything else done. But when you travel around a bit you meet a fair number of people, all with names, and it's only polite for a true gentleman to have a bit of a stab at remembering as many of those names as he possibly can.

Obviously, there are some people you'd be a complete goose if you didn't remember their name. Like if you're at a party and Barack Obama, the 44th President of the United States, is at the same party, and you leaned over to your friend and said, 'Who's the wingnut hoeing into the cheese board? He looks kinda familiar,' that would be plain wrong and the friend you're talking to would look at you like you're an idiot. If you're the 44th President of the United States, it's fair to say you'd expect people to remember your name.

But not everyone in the world is the 44th President of the United States and a lot of the people who aren't Barack Obama have names that can be tricky to remember. Like if you're Welsh, chances are your name will either have way too many l's or y's in it and be totally unpronounceable without showering them in spit; or it will be Jones. Either way, if you're stuck in a pub full of Welshmen it can be a complete nightmare, name-wise.

One of these men is going bald at a very young age.

This is where the word 'mate' is a total godsend when it comes to remembering names. This is because it takes away the whole need to remember anyone's name. They just become 'mate'. It's simple, it's easy to remember and it can get you out of many a tight spot — even in a pub full of Welshmen. And, best of all, it keeps just about everyone happy.

Ninety-nine per cent of people are happy to be called 'mate'. 'Mate' is one of the friendliest words in the whole world.

In fact, what it says is: 'Friend, I welcome you!' Even though most people will probably figure that you're trying to cover up the fact you can't remember their name, they don't mind because 'mate' is one of those words that invites you in, sits you down, puts a beer in your hand and says, 'I come in peace.'

If you encounter one of the remaining 1 per cent who object to being called 'mate' — usually some aggro bastard who wants to get all up in your face: 'You're not my mate, mate!' — then they're obviously a plonker whose name isn't worth remembering anyway, so you can hold up your hands — 'Whatever, mate' — and walk away gracefully, which is the best thing you can do to these people.

Other great things about the word 'mate' include how it can mean many different things depending on how you say it. It can be a warning if someone crosses a line they shouldn't — 'mate' — as long as you're shaking your head when you say it. Or you can say it if someone does something pretty special — 'maaaaate!' And as long as you're clear it's just what you're calling them and not what you want to do with them, you can even use it with women whose names you can't remember.

Sometimes, just for a bit of a change-up, depending on the company of course, there are other words that do the same trick as mate. 'Gorgeous' and 'bro' are a couple that spring to mind. Okay, sometimes calling a woman 'gorgeous' can get a bit borderline and it probably helps if you're an All Black to get away with it consistently, but as long as it is said with a smile (and not a pervy sort of smile) it can be an excellent icebreaker. Calling a woman 'bro' isn't generally on, except if you know them really well.

So, really, sticking to 'mate' is probably the best way to go, all up.

'Mate' — just keep it in mind and you'll be sweet in many a social situation.

BEST LOCKS I'VE EVER PLAYED WITH?

All of them, because they make me look good, but if I don't say Brad Thorn I will get in trouble.

HOW TO MEET THE QUEEN

There's this book called *Debrett's Etiquette and Modern Manners*. It's all very English and proper and is all about the 'proper' way to do stuff like eating in flash restaurants and not cocking everything up at important functions — like when you meet the Queen.

Just quietly, I don't think many (or any) of the boys have read *Debrett's Etiquette and Modern Manners*, not going on the performance levels the times I've met the Queen.

The first time I met her was on my first tour with the All Blacks, in 2002. It was a Wednesday, I think, when we got the call to put on the number ones, 'cause we're going out somewhere — they didn't tell us where to start with. Now the boys don't exactly like getting into their number ones, not midweek anyway; it's a hassle getting the suit on, tying the tie, doing the hair, the whole shebang. But after the usual round of grumbling, we all muscle up and get on the bus — which is when they tell us where we're going.

Look, I'll be honest here, some of the boys weren't exactly into this, but there were others — like me, for example — who were totally up for it. First tour with the AB's, *plus* meeting the Queen; that's not a bad result however you look at it.

So the bus gets to Buckingham Palace, and as it's waiting to get the all clear to drive in, as the bomb squad are giving it the once over, this bloke comes on board and gives us the low-down on what to do and say when we meet the Queen — probably all the stuff that's in *Debrett's Etiquette and Modern Manners* if you can be bothered reading it.

It's all the stuff about how the first time you're talking to her you're meant to call her 'Your Majesty' then after that you call her 'Ma'am' (which is pronounced 'Mam' not 'Marm' in case anyone's wondering).

The boys, of course, took all this on board, I'm sure.

Anyway, once you've got past the security and the protocol and you're actually in the palace, they whack you into this room, where there's tea and nibbly little sandwichy things with salmon on them, on fancy plates. And everyone spreads out, not entirely sure what to

Her picture doesn't do her justice. She is way hotter in real life. Chris Jack is also looking not too shabby.

do, what the form is here. Then this odd English bloke — a footman or something, I don't know what his official title is, so we'll call him Royal Tea Guy — comes over and asks us if we want tea. Sure, says everyone, why not? So Royal Tea Guy picks up the pot to start serving, then realises it is insanely hot and drops it back down.

'Fuck!' says Royal Tea Guy.

Now I don't know whether Royal Tea Guy does the same thing for all visiting sports teams, just to break the ice, but it sure worked for us because the moment he said 'Fuck!' everyone cracked up and relaxed totally.

So, feeling much better about things, the boys make a beeline

'Where have you been all my life?'

for the little salmon sandwichy things, and start hoeing into them.

And they were really horrible.

So now everyone's standing round with the half-eaten food wondering what the protocol is for quietly dumping it somewhere without offending the Royal Sandwich-making Person and getting charged with treason or something, when the doors open and all these corgis come charging in.

For a few seconds the boys are all standing there, wondering where the hell these little bastards came from, then they realise that the corgis are totally into the salmon sandwichy things. Problem solved, and pretty soon there are All Blacks all over the show, feeding the corgis.

Which, of course, is when Her Majesty the Queen walks in, along with her hubby, Prince Philip.

Now if she thought, 'Why are all these large men poisoning my dogs?' she didn't actually say anything as everyone ditched the food and formed up for the official greetings. Taine Randell, as captain, is doing the duty, taking her round the room introducing her and Phil to everyone. We're all standing in little groups, waiting.

The first thing you notice about the Queen is how unbelievably tiny she is.

I know I'm tall, but at the other end of the scale is her — really, really short. It's lucky she's the Queen and has all these people round her because if she didn't she'd keep getting knocked over because no-one would notice she's there. She'd be useless in a nightclub — you'd never be able to see she was there.

Now it turned out, because of the way she was going round the room, that I was in the last group that was going to meet her. And in the group with me was Keith Robinson, also on his first tour with the ABs. Now Keith is no oil painting, but he's a really good bloke — and he's for certain much more at home out pig-hunting than in Buckingham Palace, meeting the Queen.

So Her Majesty finally gets to us and I'm the first in line now, and Taine does the intros and I lean down so I'm within earshot and say something along the lines of 'Lovely to meet you, Your Majesty' — which I thought was pretty admirable under the circumstances. And she says something Queen-like and moves on to the next person, and then to the next.

Until, eventually, she gets to Keith.

Now I don't know if she was thrown by Keith's beauty, but for some reason she kind of stopped in her tracks — just for a second — looking at him. And for a second they're just standing there, looking at each other. Meanwhile you can see Keith's brain ticking over: 'Why the hell isn't she saying hello to me?' And so, as the pause gets a bit longer, Keith decides to take matters into his own hands.

'How's it going, love?' says Keith, to Her Majesty the Queen.

The Queen, to her credit, as the bunch of supposedly grown men standing around her try real hard not to crack up and giggle like little girls, took this breach of protocol remarkably well.

'Oh, very nice, very nice, thank you,' said the Queen, with a little smile on her face.

At which point in time Keith decides that his next move will be to thrust out a big, pig-hunting mitt, to shake hands with the ruling monarch. The Queen, again to her credit, holds out her hand — this tiny, tiny hand — and they shake.

All I have to say is that the Queen might be bloody small but she must also be bloody tough, as she survived the full-body shaking that Keith gave her as he pumped his mitt up and down. It was priceless.

I'm sure, once the Royal Physio had put her spine back in the right place, that the Queen quite likes meeting blokes like Keith; that it'd liven up her day. I've been told that she really likes meeting the All Blacks — she doesn't have to do it, but she really likes doing it. Mind you, that might have all changed after the last time she met me and Ross Filipo on the 2008 end-of-year tour.

Keith Robinson can only watch in awe as I work my magic with the ladies.

This time she came to us, 'cause we were in a park in the middle of London, standing in the freezing cold, alongside the monster Tourism New Zealand rugby ball. And the Queen turns up, with the Prime Minister in tow and we all head inside, into the ball, to watch a movie about New Zealand — which only makes Ross homesick, which probably goes part way to explaining what he said after the film.

Again Her Majesty is doing the rounds, meeting and greeting the boys, but when she gets to Flossy, instead of sticking to what you'd find in *Debrett's Etiquette and Modern Manners* he goes and asks her if she fancies popping over to New Zealand for a barbecue at his place. Not, I would guess, an invite the Queen gets every day of the week.

Which means by the time she gets to me the Queen is probably completely over these big, tall clowns from New Zealand. Not that this prevents me from adding to proceedings by making a further idiot out of myself.

'Is this your first time in London?' the Queen asks me, after we've exchanged opening pleasantries.

'Well, it's not actually,' I say to her. 'Actually this is the third time we've met. In fact, third time, I would consider this more like our first actual date.'

And she gives me a look that translates in any country and any language as 'what a goose', then gives me a polite little chuckle and moves on, quick smart. When she got back to the Palace I reckon she might have checked to see if she still had the power to behead people who talked bollocks at her.

Yeah, I reckon after Keith, Flossy and me, that Her Majesty the Queen has probably had a gutsful of All Black locks.

HOW (NOT) TO CELEBRATE
IN STYLE #1

Having a few quiet ales, with comrades and friends, is an acceptable way to celebrate anything, at any time, even if there's nothing really to celebrate. There's nothing wrong with a few quiet ales. It's what happens after the few quiet ales turn into a few more quiet ales where things can start to turn tricky and some serious explaining might need to be done.

The ways things can go horribly wrong after a few quiet ales are many. Ending up wearing totally inappropriate clothing with no real idea why, is one. Waking up with a haircut you can really live without and can't remember getting is another. Making not entirely serious phone calls while pretending to be someone else can also be a recipe for disaster — especially if the person on the other end of the phone twigs you've had a few quiet ones and isn't thrilled to be drunk-dialled.

Man-hugging: a more traditional way of celebrating victory, but only half the fun.

But this story is about none of those things. This is the story of how, on the end-of-year tour 2005, I ended up *not* playing against Wales.

So it's a Sunday afternoon, the day after Auckland had beaten Otago 39–11 to win the last ever NPC title, before it got turned into the Air New Zealand Cup, before they restructure everything again and turn it into something called something else but which isn't that different from what they had before.

Anyway, we'd won the NPC and as part of the ongoing celebrations we're all having a few quiet ales and some tofu pizza at Eden Park on a Sunday afternoon.

And when you're at Eden Park, and you've had a few quiet ones, and the place is empty, eventually someone suggests a game of touch footie — I mean, the pitch is just sitting there, begging to be used, right? And then, inevitably, someone proposes an amendment to the way touch footie is usually played; and you all think, 'Why the hell not?' and then one thing leads to another and pretty soon there are a couple of grown men, who should probably know better, clowning around on the hallowed turf.

With no clothes on.

I'll probably get in trouble for saying this, like I get in trouble most times I open my mouth, but streaking has been a tradition at many sporting venues, for many years now. It is, you might say, a part of the game. And traditions need to be honoured, from time to time.

Now it's not like I'm encouraging all the clowns out there who feel the need to get their kit off and run onto the pitch in the middle of a game just to try to get on TV. I reckon there's a world of difference between a bloke munted enough to get naked in sub-zero temperatures at Carisbrook in the middle of winter, or some publicity hound in a bikini, and a bunch of blokes in peak physical condition enjoying a Sunday afternoon game of footie as a tribute to all those streakers who have set foot on Eden Park over the years.

Also, like I say, we'd had a few quiet ones.

Anyway, there we are, me and a team-mate who shall remain nameless for now, feeling the wind on our skin and all that, indulging in a bit of harmless fun on a Sunday afternoon. After a while, we're just about to pack it in, but I need one last try to seal the deal, so I decide to take him on round the outside; the plan being to make a beeline for the corner and dive over in a blaze of naked glory.

Nice plan. And for a moment there, I had him, until I realised that, in my time of need, my top-end speed had deserted me.

And so the big dive for the corner ended up short.

Closely followed by the also agonising realisation that, in the process, I'd managed to bugger up my shoulder; completely rooted the AC joint, as it would turn out.

Anyway, so there I am — all the beneficial effects of the few quiet ones long gone in favour of a bloody sore shoulder. To top things off, I'm stark naked on the pitch at Eden Park and all my clothes are right at the top of the terraces, so I have to walk all the way up through the empty stands, with a busted wing and not a lot of sympathy from my fellow players, get dressed, get a taxi out of there. From there it's straight home and straight to bed, feeling like a total wally.

I'm not very good at thinking ahead at the best of times, but this time it was special because the next day I had to assemble with the rest of the team for the AB's end-of-year tour, starting with the test against Wales in three weeks. Three weeks is not a long time when it comes to injured AC joints. So, basically, as I assemble with the rest of the touring party I'm thinking, 'This isn't going to go down so well.'

'Come on, Shag, lighten up. There's only so many ways a bloke can say sorry.'

I was right. It didn't. Not even with me trying to play it cool.

Pretty soon I have to front up to Shag, aka Steve Hansen, and the conversation goes something like this:

'Okay mate, so what happened?'

'Mate, it happened in the game,' I say.

'That's one chance,' he says.

'What do you mean?'

'You've got three chances. You just used one of them.'

'Oh, okay,' I go. 'Yeah, we were clowning around and I tripped over.'

'Okay, that's another chance gone. You've got one more.'

'One more chance 'til what?'

'Chance to tell me what really happened. If you don't tell me what really happened, you're not coming on tour.'

'You can't do that.'

'I can do whatever I want.'

And he wasn't joking. That was the most painful part of proceedings. Part of the reason Shag is such a great guy is that he doesn't piss around. Yeah, some of his pre-match motivational speeches are a bit hard to fathom, but when he's being straight up with you, he expects the same in return. This didn't leave me with exactly too many options.

'Alright, I was nude and we were playing a bit of a touch game, you know how boys do, eh? And then one of the boys tackled me in the corner and this is what happened.'

And he looked at me for an age, clearly trying to understand what kind of goose would do something so stupid, the day before an All Black tour, before he shook his head and sighed.

'Yeah, okay. I accept that. You can come.'

So I missed the first test, against Wales, and played the rest of the tests with some assistance from the medical staff. Officially, the story went out that I sustained the injury in a game of 'backyard rugby'. Personally, I like to think of Eden Park as almost being like my backyard so I can work with that.

HOW (NOT) TO CELEBRATE IN STYLE #2

2002 was my second season in the Auckland NPC team, and we hadn't exactly got off to a flying start. We'd lost to Taranaki at Eden Park in the first game and by the time we were seven games into the season we'd also managed to lose to Canterbury and Waikato, so things weren't looking too flash all round.

Anyway, there are just a couple of games to go in the round-robin, part of the competition and I'm talking to a certain bloke (who should probably remain nameless) and we get onto the subject of Viagra. Let's just say that when you're a young bloke you're curious about this sort of stuff and leave it at that.

So after some discussion about the effects and use of Viagra with the unnamed chap, a bet is proposed, along the lines of: 'if we win this thing, you've got to get the boys some of this stuff to try'. The bloke, who is feeling pretty confident that we are way off the pace and not even going to make the semi-finals, is up for this. Game on.

We beat Otago in the second to last game, then monster Wellington 47–24 down in the capital to make it into third place on the table. In the semi we take out Canterbury, 29–23, down in Christchurch. Then it's down to Hamilton to account for Waikato, 40–28, in the final.

So Auckland are the 2002 NPC champions and there is one bloke who owes the boys a big favour.

But being a man of his word, the bloke comes through with the magic pills for the boys — and they are bloody well handed out pretty much straight after the game, when the celebrations are just

Me, Scott Palmer and rules expert Daniel Braid — before the pills kicked in.
(P.S. Anyone who says Scott Palmer is overweight is lying.)

kicking into gear. (I hate to think what he was planning to do with them if we'd lost.)

So, with boys being boys, the prevailing thought going round is: 'like hell am I going to leave this in my back pocket all night'. And then one thing leads to another and at least half a dozen tabs of Viagra are being emptied, on the sly, into the NPC trophy, which is full of beer, doing the traditional rounds of the team, with everyone drinking from it.

So the scene goes something like this: team is drinking the Viagra-laced beer from the NPC trophy — which is probably not entirely respectful to the competition, but what's done is done, eh? And anyone who comes and joins in the team celebrations is drinking from the trophy, as is the tradition. And one of the people drinking from the trophy, not knowing at the time about its special super-powers, is Ted, aka Graham Henry, the future All Black coach.

Now I don't want to dwell on what may or may not have happened with Ted later on that night — it turns out Viagra and beer doesn't work for everyone — but I do recall a few of my team-mates saying things along the lines of: 'Bloody hell, what's going on here?' One guy, at about 1am, comes up to me going 'Shit, this is ridiculous. I can't get rid of this bastard.' He had to disappear for an hour or so, to sort himself out.

I haven't done the maths to see if, nine months later, there were any unexpected surprises as a result of the Viagra/NPC trophy/beer incident. And, like I said, it's probably not the ideal way of respectfully crowning a winning season, but boys will be boys, eh? Sometimes for longer than usual.

I have no idea what these are or what you use them for.

THE MAIN
DIFFERENCE BETWEEN
MEN AND WOMEN

It is a proven fact (at least around my house) that the main difference between men and women (apart from the obvious ones) is channel surfing.

For example, women believe that advertising breaks in television programmes are there so you can turn the sound down and talk about stuff. Men, on the other hand, know for a fact that the only reason advertising breaks are there is so that you can surf around as many channels as humanly possible, just to check if you're missing something better.

Women have no concept of the basic human male need for channel surfing. It is important to know what is on every available TV channel, as often as you can. It's the male hunting instinct at work, except it happens to be lying down on the couch with a remote in its hand, instead of being out on the tundra hunting woolly mammoths.

FUN WITH THE MEDIA

I'm not saying I had any part in this. I'm not even saying I was on the same flight. Okay, I was on the same flight, but I'm still not saying it had anything to do with me. There are heaps of culprits at work here, so to single me out would be wrong. I'm just getting that down on paper, for the record, okay?

One of the things that can be a real pain in the arse when you're an All Black is that sometimes people really, truly want to spend time with you. I guess it's the downside of the power of the jersey, that there are people out there who want to hang with you, if they're given the opportunity, for way longer than they should. I mean, it's cool wanting to be one of the boys and to be with the boys, but there comes a time when it's a case of: 'you've had your fun now, time to move on, mate'.

But there are some people who don't realise when their time is up and who just don't know how to take a hint.

We were in South Africa, just about to head home, when this

79

bloke — let's call him The Man from the Media — caught up with us while we were doing some shopping (some of the boys really like their shopping, just quietly) before getting on the plane. And he starts telling us about this charity fight he had with another Man from the Media, talking himself up to us, big time. And it's all, like, 'I just kept lining him up — booyah, booyah!' That was his catchphrase: 'Booyah!'

But it's all cool to start off with, and we're having lunch before we get on the plane, a couple of quiet ones, as you do. And The Man from the Media comes along. Booyah! And it's all good fun through lunch — booyah, booyah! And he buys everyone a round, which is very hospitable of him, but after a while the whole 'booyah!' thing starts to get a bit tired. But we've got a plane to catch, so we buy him a chilli-vodka shot, as a goodbye present — which, to his credit, he hoovered down — and we head our separate ways.

Or so we thought.

Until, it turns out that he's upgraded himself to Business Class to have a few more beers with the boys on the way home. Booyah. And there is no escape from the booyah when you're stuck in an aeroplane for many, many hours.

Okay, what happened next is for certain nothing to be proud of, but desperate times call for desperate measures because the booyah booyah booyah at altitude, for a long time, is not an ideal way to travel. So, basically, what we did was we got one of the air crew to keep bringing us beers. And we kept feeding The Man from the Media beers. Many beers. Many, many beers.

Until, finally, the booyah was silenced. He's coma'd out in his seat. No more booyah.

But now it's time for a little payback.

First of all, he looked kinda uncomfortable, sleeping there, in all his clothes, so most of them had to go. So they did.

Naturally, what came next was the thought that when you've got a Man from the Media, coma'd out, just lying there, a bit of facial decoration is certainly called for. Just to improve his TV good looks, of course. Nothing sinister, just a few temporary tattoos, as it were. Maybe a moko, just to try it out, see if it suited him.

And then, when you've gone that far, eventually you look at the new and improved Man from the Media, still sound asleep, and you think, 'We may as well, eh?'

So it's out with the shaving cream and the razor and off comes the eyebrow. Just the one. Just to see what he'd look like; see if maybe he'd like it. Booyah.

Eventually, of course, The Man from the Media wakes up, when we're coming into Sydney — because you have to stop off in Oz when you're flying back from South Africa. And he starts thinking something untoward has gone on as he gets his clothes back in order, but he hasn't twigged to the face-painting and the eyebrow thing yet. Meanwhile the boys are all trying not to crack up as he heads off to the toilets to get himself sorted before we land.

Now obviously I don't know exactly what went on in that toilet when he caught sight of himself in the mirror, but I bet the language was probably more out of *Outrageous Fortune* than the sort of stuff The Man from the Media does for a living. I know if it was me, I'd have been slutted beyond all belief.

Anyway, by the time he came out of the bog, he'd managed

to scrub most of the stuff off his face, but: (a) now his face was bright red; and (b) if he'd noticed the lack of the eyebrow, he didn't let on. Maybe, with the scrubbing and the monster hangover that was probably starting to kick in, his brain hadn't registered the extent of the damage yet.

But eventually he must have, because The Man from the Media didn't appear on the telly for a couple of weeks after that. And then when he did, if you looked real carefully — and you were in the know about what had gone on during that flight — you could tell that the other eyebrow was drawn on.

Like I said, it's probably nothing to be proud of, but every now and then you meet someone who just cries out to be stitched up. Booyah!

BEST TEAM I'VE EVER PLAYED IN?

Western Springs Swans — soccer Under-5s.

BEST TEAM I'VE EVER PLAYED AGAINST?

Western Springs Swans (Blue) — soccer Under-5s.

DIFFERENT SHAPED PEGS, DIFFERENT SHAPED HOLES

There's this tendency to treat the All Blacks as though being an All Black turns you into something that should behave in a certain way and fits into this idea the public — and especially the media — seem to have about what an All Black should be.

Even putting aside my own personal problems fitting into the appropriate stereotype for anything and everything, let alone doing what an All Black should do and say, I still reckon it's impossible to lump all these people from different cultural backgrounds and different life situations together, call them All Blacks and then expect them all to behave in a certain way.

How can you expect, to use a pretty basic example, guys who are married with kids and happy with their lot, to be the same All Blacks as young single guys who want to see what wearing the fern does for them on a night out on the town? Can't be done, I reckon.

What unites the All Blacks happens on the field and in the

Insert your own 'who farted?' joke here.

times when you're together as a team trying to do what you do best. I think the All Black management is really good at recognising the differences in all the guys, and in managing things so that there's a culture of acceptance within the team; of respecting whatever people need to do personally to enjoy this amazing time of their lives.

Obviously, there are limits, but there is also huge acceptance of what the individual needs to function — within the structure the All Black management has in place.

It's generally when the guys are outside this structure, out in public, when you're not on duty, that the trouble starts. And then suddenly, when the shit has hit the fan and you've ended up in the papers, it's not just you getting caught behaving like a goose, suddenly it becomes the whole All Black culture that's on trial. That's wrong, in my book (which is what this book is) and it's not fair on the individuals or the team.

So what that the guys want to go out and have a good time? Why should it make any difference what colour shirt you wear on some nights of the year?

And that's all I have to say on the matter.

At least until the next time I have something to say on the matter.

BUS
ETIQUETTE

There was this All Black ad once, in association with the kind people at Ford, where the team bus had broken down and a whole bunch of the boys had to hitchhike to the game. This story is a bit like that, only I don't think they'd ever use what happened on this bus trip to advertise anything.

It is an uplifting story nonetheless; a story of inventiveness and determination. It ends with a victory for the little guy after he has been wrongfully accused of trouble-making and has been cast into the wilderness by his own team-mates.

It begins, as these stories often do, with an end-of-season social gathering; this time of the Blues. In this instance of social shenanigans, it's a bus tour taking in the many and varied locales within the Blues franchise area; and taking in some of the many and varied forms of hospitality on offer at said locales along the way. Needless to say it's a lively affair that gets livelier as the tour progresses.

As with all rugby teams there are certain rules when it comes to transport by bus, and this day was certainly no exception. Many of these rules revolve around the back seat of the bus and, specifically, who gets to sit there. Again, this day was no exception; the back seat belongs to the most senior of senior players and only they shall park their arses there.

What was different about this day is that, on this bus, the back seat is up for grabs. If some young buck thinks he has the stones to take a rightful place on the back seat, he may do so: as long as he

Mike Cron and some idiot. One of these men had a big night the night before.

ousts someone who already has their arse planted on that seat. This can only be done by force, by physically removing the most senior of senior players from the seat and taking his place. Think of it like one of those nature documentaries on TV where the two mountain goats or whatever go at it, head to head, until one goat walks away and one goat stands victorious – only we're not goats; and we're on a bus, not a mountain; and the winner will be sitting down, not standing. But you get what I mean.

Now, believe it or not, I'm not quite among the most senior of senior players among the Blues squad (bring on 2010, I say) but, as a senior player but not quite senior enough to be actually on the back seat, but a senior player nonetheless, defending that back seat was my sacred duty. I was the castle the young buck must first conquer, if he wants a crack at the back seat.

Anyway, to go down the Tana Route, obviously what is happening at the back of the bus is not tiddlywinks.

These are big guys, going at it hammer and tongs, trying to get past me, at the back seat. You're not exactly belting each other, but you're sure as hell not letting the other guy past so it's not exactly, to go down another Tana route, whacking each other over the head with handbags either. 'Carnage' is as good a word as any to describe it, I reckon.

So, having set the scene, it is time to get back to this particular bus trip. We'd made our way, from memory (which I have to confess may not be entirely reliable), through Takapuna and

89

around various parts of the North Shore, until we landed, I think, somewhere in the general vicinity of Albany or possibly Silverdale; I'm not too flash when it comes to geography, especially on a day where everyone is cutting loose. It was there that the challenge was thrown down and one of the young crew made his move on the seat.

So we start at it. I'm not letting him pass and he's not backing down in a hurry, so it's turning into a fairly full-on scuffle, down at the back of the bus.

Meanwhile, up at the front of the bus, the bus-driver, Grant (aka Grunter) is looking at this carry-on, horrified. This is not the way grown men behave — not on his bus. So, or so I heard later, Grunter talks to the management blokes up the front, basically saying, 'Sort this shit out, I don't want this sort of shit on my bus.' But the management explain to him that this is the way it is on this particular outing — it's just guys letting off steam, having a bit of fun.

But Grunter — who, I might add, is actually a top bloke — isn't buying this for a dollar. So he marches down the bus and gets our attention by, basically, standing there shouting at us until we stop fighting. And he lets us know in no uncertain terms what he thinks of this carry-on, then he points the finger at me and says, 'You, off the bus.'

Now at first I'm not sure: (a) I'm hearing right and (b) why the hell I'm getting the finger pointed at me when all I was doing was defending what was rightfully mine. But Grunter isn't kidding and the ultimatum is either Williams gets off the bus or the bus isn't going anywhere anytime soon.

So, being a good boy who always does what he's told — and because my team-mates were not so much 'leaping to my defence' as more 'cheering and laughing their arses off' — I got off the bus.

And then the bus drove away, heading off to Silverdale or Albany or wherever (as I said before, the details escape me), the next stop on the tiki tour. The last thing I see is a bunch of blokes giving me the fingers from the back seat — the seat that I was wrongfully sent from the bus for defending. What a pack of ungrateful bastards.

Meanwhile there am I, all alone, by the side of the road, surveying my options. The most obvious one would seem to be 'call a taxi, go home', but like hell am I giving it away that easy. Like hell am I going to let those bastards get away with this.

So out goes the thumb. I know where the bus is heading and I will get there, come hell or high water. No way are they getting rid of Ali Williams that easy, not when there's serious drinking to be done.

And just like the ad on TV, this guy sees this big galah standing on the side of the road, trying to cadge a ride, and he pulls over. I tell him where I need to be and he says, 'No problems, Ali,' and I climb onto the back tray of his ute and it's away we go.

Probably the most satisfying thing about this whole story is that not only did this guy, a saint if ever I met one, get me to where I needed to be, but we managed to overtake the bus on the way there. Let me tell you that the satisfaction of giving the finger to a bunch of bastards who have abandoned you, as you cruise past them on the motorway, is pretty much second to none.

By the time the bus pulled into the next designated hospitality location, not only am I already there, sipping a quiet beer, but I've befriended a road crew who were there and they have kindly lent me one of their fluoro vests, just so the boys won't miss me when they walk in.

And when eventually they do, I raise a glass to them in the traditional manner and give them my best shit-eating grin — 'What kept you, boys?'

Fast forward a few hours, when it's time to take the tired and emotional crew home, and who should be sitting back in his rightful place, up near the back of the bus — a little shabby round the edges, that's for sure, but back where he belongs?

Yeah, you got it: the hitchhiking man, that's who.

BEST HAIRCUT EVER?

Joe Dirt.

WORST HAIRCUT EVER?

Richie McCaw.

AFTER IT ALL WENT PEAR-SHAPED

France 20, New Zealand 18.

Bollocks.

It wasn't meant to end like this; not at the quarter-finals; not to the French who broke my bloody jaw as well; not by becoming the worst performed New Zealand team at any Rugby World Cup. Not after I gave up potato chips for this.

Okay, on the face of it that doesn't sound like much, but I love potato chips and I'll easily hoe through a whole bag — a big bag, mind you, not just one of those little ones — two or three times a week. And I gave that up; along with other stuff I love, like salami and bacon, to train my arse off. When a man gives up bacon for his country, you know he means business.

And then it all went pear-shaped.

I don't want to go down the road of refereeing performances or where it actually all went wrong, in a finger-pointing sense. It's

fair enough to say, I think, that if the game was a disaster, then the aftermath was a nightmare; a total bloody nightmare; when you're thinking that the whole nation must hate you. I remember I was back in my room at The Vale, where we were based, outside Cardiff; I was in my room and my phone was sitting there and there was a text, I can't remember who it was from or what it said, it was some silly text from one of my mates, and I thought 'I don't need this shit, I just want to block myself out from the world, from that world back home.'

So I picked up the phone and threw it against the wall. Boom! Gone. Let it go.

The next day, when I finally woke up and got it together enough to think I better phone the missus, I realised the phone was in pieces on the floor — whoops. Luckily, all the pieces went back together in the right order and they apparently make mobile phones tougher than you think. So I was able to return it to a functioning state and turn it on; and the phone went mental. Beep beep beep beep beep beep beep beep! There were something like 27 texts waiting for me.

So I started reading them, and they were mainly along the lines of: 'What the hell were you doing losing, you useless prick?' and 'Do you know how much shit the police are dealing with here because of you?' and heaps of stuff along those lines. And I was reading them going 'What the hell? I don't need all this crap!'

And then I started to laugh, because they were all from my mates — mainly my mates outside of rugby — winding me up. It was not

Okay, that didn't go quite how we planned it.

pleasant at first, but it helped to start to put things in perspective. The game was a shambles; everything you'd worked towards for ages was down the toilet; but afterwards you still had your mates to give you arseholes when you least wanted it, but probably most needed it.

There's this room at The Vale, this sort of underground premises within the place, which the team took over, where we eventually gathered so we could be together, as a team, with friends and family. It was somewhere where we could lock ourselves away from the rest of the world; maybe have a few quiet ones to help dull the pain.

> But everything was dead; everyone was just dead. It was like the worst thing in the world had happened and we were at the centre of it.

Something drastic was needed to put everything in perspective. It was time for the team clown to step up.

Being a bloke to never shy away from dressing up in order to break the ice at a party (even a wake) I went into the toilet with a whole bunch of tape and compression bandages; and I started taping myself up. All over the show — legs, arms, body, head, but remembering to leave a hole for my mouth so I could still drink my beer. By the time I was finished, I looked like this deranged version of something out of *The Mummy*.

Suitably attired, I crashed out of the bathroom and waded in

'Did I miss something? Why do I have this feeling we just screwed up monumentally?'

among the boys, doing my best 'just out of the crypt' impersonation, to remind everyone there are worse things than losing a rugby match; like being dead for example — or possibly having this raving lunatic wrapped in bandages making a dick of himself in front of you. And it worked, I reckon, and the mood lifted noticeably — I mean, how could it not?

But after about 15 minutes of this, the deed had been done and it was time to slip back into the bathroom, get rid of the tape and the bandages, and turn back into my normal self. And this was when I really discovered that (surprise, surprise) I hadn't thought things through 110 per cent, because getting the bloody tape off my body was, if you'll pardon the language, fucking painful. It took me about half an hour to get it all off and by the time I'd finished my body was bright red. Not a great look in anyone's book.

But at least things had perked up, to the extent where the guitars had come out and a few songs were being sung — and a few beers were being sunk. Which is when the Honky Tonk Man made his appearance.

I'm not going to say too much about the true identity of the Honky Tonk Man — except to say it definitely wasn't me. What he and I shared, that night, was a willingness to try to lift the spirits of the boys in the hour of greatest darkness, but we went about it in very different ways: I managed to rip large chunks of hair and a layer of skin from my body; he picked up someone else's guitar and entertained everyone with a few tunes. The fact that it was 'someone else's guitar' comes into play a bit later on.

So the Honky Tonk Man is doing his honky tonk thing, playing up a storm for the boys. While he's doing this, and everyone is cheering him on, one of our media guys is trying to round up some people to go and talk to the press because, you know, we've just

'Play "Stairway to Heaven"!'

lost at the quarter-final stage of the Rugby World Cup and so on. But when he tries to persuade the Honky Tonk Man to front up and do the duty, the Honky Tonk Man isn't having a bar of it — and neither are the rest of the guys, who want the Honky Tonk Man to carry on doing that thing that he's doing so well. Media access denied.

Which let the Honky Tonk Man off the hook — and off the hook he was. The Honky Tonk Man was working the room, right up to the point where the Honky Tonk Man announced to everyone that

'This is what I do!' At which time he took the guitar and brought it down, hard, on the head of one of the boys.

Which was not good.

The forward didn't mind; in fact he didn't really notice the guitar getting totalled around his skull. If the truth be known, which in this case is probably not the best idea, us forwards are pretty resilient like that.

No, it was more the fact that the guitar the Honky Tonk Man had just trashed belonged to the same media guy who was getting frustrated at the lack of interview cooperation that caused the trouble which ensued. There were some fairly hasty team discussions that followed and the whole matter just added to the craziness building around this whole experience.

And then the hair cutting started.

At this point in time I was crafting a whole mullet thing; doing the business at the front, letting it party at the back. It was no Jason

Eaton but it was developing nicely, with a bit of a rat's tail down there, because that's the way it went and I was happy to let nature take its course. I told everyone I wasn't cutting it because it gave me super-powers, like Samson.

Keith Robinson is clearly not a believer in the Power of the Mullet because that night he took up some scissors, stepped up behind me and while I was otherwise distracted, he chopped the tail off the rat. I was gutted.

'What'd you do that for, man? Why'd you cut Samson? I've got no powers now!'

'Yeah, your powers worked out real well, didn't they?' he said.

There was no argument to that. And from there on in the scissors were put to use and a lot of impromptu hair cutting followed. It might have gone a lot better if it had been Neemia Tialata manning the scissors because he does a proper job. Neemia is, just for the record, an awesome barber. I would — and from time to time do — entrust my hair to that man. Graham Henry entrusts what little hair he has left to that man. But that night Neemia let butchers like Keith Robinson — who has no hair and therefore escaped the carnage — take up the scissors and do the cutting. Not pretty; really not pretty.

All of which helped numb the pain after everything the boys had done, all the sacrifices they'd made for what turned out to be a nightmare of monumental proportions. We came back home, we walked around with our heads down for a while; and then we got on with life, because that's what you do.

And the story of the weekend at Raglan, dealing with everything just after the return, and the David Bain inspired op-shop jerseys is, I'm afraid, a story for another book.

A SIMPLE PHILOSOPHY
PART 1

If you're hungry, you eat. If you're thirsty, you drink. If you need to shit, well . . . you get the picture. This is a philosophy handed down to me by a bloke I'd call a great mate and something of a mentor — my fishing buddy Geoff Thomas. A top man all round and a great advocate of the motto: life, when you boil it down to the basics, is pretty bloody simple.

But the way people look at things, look at life, they start complicating everything. When's the right time for me to eat? What should I eat? How much of whatever I have to eat is right for me to eat? Before you know it you're beating yourself up and you haven't even eaten yet. If you want to eat, eat. If you're worried that you've eaten too much, go for a run. Are you tired after all that eating and running? Go to sleep.

Geoff Thomas, some bloke with one giant ab and Lee Wynyard (in need of a haircut).

Being a professional sportsman these days means you're always going to have people around you, helping you make pretty basic decisions in life. It keeps the organisation happy and, for some people, it's obviously good that they've got this support. But, for me, the line I walk is pretty straight; I just like to walk it in my own way.

Like, if a nutritionist says I need to eat four bananas a day, no one can force me to eat the four bananas. I need to look at the whole banana issue and decide for myself whether the four bananas thing will get me what I want; not because someone says it will.

If I want to look in the mirror and go, 'Woof, you sexy hunk', and I reckon the bananas can get me there, then sign me up.

To win the Rugby World Cup, I may even go to five or six bananas a day, if *I* accept what the pro-banana people are telling me and then *I* decide that's what it will take.

Like they say: you can lead a horse to water but you can't make him buy you a drink — or eat a banana.

Or something along those lines.

HOW TO CATCH MANY FISH

Go out fishing for several days. Do not wash, do not change your clothes, forget everything you know about personal hygiene. Get as smelly as humanly possible; go totally feral on it.

The sea will reward you with many, many fish. If that doesn't work, try a long-line.

A SIMPLE PHILOSOPHY
PART 2

I'll admit that I came to rugby late and for all the wrong reasons. I used to play every other sport under the sun, but I really wanted to be a professional soccer player; a striker, preferably. Then, as I kept growing and kept getting more unco, they kept shifting me further back down the field until I ended up in goal. Which is about when I realised that it was the guys in the 1st XV who got all the hottest girls, at which time my interest in soccer waned and my interest in rugby took off.

After that stunning realisation it became all about hard work — and luck. And that's what I reckon a lot of life is a mix of: work and luck. Once I got the desire to be a rugby player and to play at the highest level, I worked my arse off trying to fulfil that desire.

Yeah, I know I've had some lucky breaks in my career. I'm aware

Jay Williams, a way more naturally gifted player than Ali Williams.

of this every day, when I look at the road my brother, Jay, has taken — and it's, like, four times, or five or six times, as long as mine was. I used to watch him, trying to marry up an engineering degree and a job with a rugby career — training at six in the morning, just to try and fit it all in.

And to top it all off, there was me, getting in his way; competing for the same position — and even though, just quietly, I reckon Jay's a way more naturally gifted player than me, I was the one getting the nod from the coaches. I was the one getting the lucky breaks.

To Jay's eternal credit, I don't think he got pissed off about that. I mean, he probably did but he never let on to me; he just hung with his mates and carried on doing what he was doing, following his own path.

The first time Jay and I ever played first class rugby together was when I was coming back from the broken jaw in 2007. It was against Bay of Plenty in the Air New Zealand Cup; we won 41–3. This was stellar compared to the first time we started a Super 14 match together for the Blues, against the Hurricanes. We got hammered and I lasted 17 minutes before the Achilles gave out and that was it for me for 2009.

I'm glad Jay and I ended up in the same Blues squad. It's good to have your brother alongside you — and that our different paths ended up at the same spot. Also, if I'm playing in the same team as him, rather than against him, the little bastard can't get any cheap shots in at the clean-out like he did when the Chiefs played the Crusaders in 2008, when he nailed me, big time.

You want another simple philosophy from a simple rugby player, try this one for size: in the end it comes down to this simple fact — live life. Find a way that sits with you and follow it with everything your heart desires. Throw the bloody kitchen sink at it — and then hope for luck.

Oh and just to set the record straight, Jay might be a more naturally gifted player than me, but I got the good looks in the family.

Ali Williams, much better looking than Jay Williams.

BEST LOCKS I'VE EVER PLAYED AGAINST?

Victor Matfield (Bulls and South Africa); Nathan Sharpe (Western Force and Australia); Martin Johnson (Leicester and England) — because the bastards are all better than me.

A SIGN OF THINGS TO COME

Isn't it funny how sometimes people, people who don't know you from Adam, can see things in you way before you see the same thing in yourself?

I was playing for the Auckland Under-13 soccer team; in goal, complete with blue hair, to show how proud I was of my province. I have no idea who it was we were playing, but in the process of stopping one of their strikers, the other kid managed to stand on my nuts.

He didn't mean to stand on my nuts, but the fact remained that he did stand on my nuts and I wasn't entirely thrilled at having my nuts stood on. My nuts were important to me back then, as they remain important to me to this very day.

Look at the form! To think I could have been an All White.

109

Thus I really didn't take having my nuts stood upon very well and I proceeded to chase the kid who had done it, trying to clout him. By the time I'd chased him to the halfway line the referee was in a position to intervene and ask me what the hell I thought I was doing.

I told him about the nut-standing and of my deep desire to bash the kid who had done it. The referee looked at me like I was a complete moron (in much the same way some referees still look at me, even to this day).

'Buddy,' he said, 'you are so playing the wrong sport. Maybe you should try rugby.'

Of course, since changing codes and playing rugby for a fair few years now, I have had these same nuts walked upon many times, but I tend not to chase after the offenders any more – mainly because they tend less to run away and more to standing there and taking a swing at me when they seeing me coming. And, quite frankly, the risk of copping it both in the nuts *and* the head hardly seems worth the bother these days.

It's enough to bring tears to a man's eye.

A RECIPE FOR BURGER SOUP

INGREDIENTS:

2 x beef, avocado and bacon burgers
milk

1. Break jaw, thus making it physically impossible to eat solid food.

2. Live on a diet of soup and smoothies for several weeks or until you are sick of eating soup and smoothies, whichever comes first.

3. Start to crave meat like you wouldn't believe. Everywhere you go, everyone around you is eating actual proper food, especially meat.

4. Go slightly bonkers, what with the meat cravings and all.

5. Eat soup and try to imagine it is a burger.

6.   Fail miserably at Step 5; possibly even shed a tear or two as meat cravings worsen.

7.   Have genius idea.

8.   Walk up to nearest Burger Wisconsin outlet, handily not too far from house.

9.   Through wired up jaw, order two beef, avocado and bacon burgers – to go.

10.   Hurry back to house, clutching beef, avocado and bacon burgers.

11.   Place both beef, avocado and bacon burgers in blender. (Remember to take burgers out of paper bag first.)

12.   Put lid on blender and turn on high.

13.   Blend the hell out of burgers until well blended.

14.   Look at resulting mixture and think, 'I'll never get that through a straw.'

15.   Add milk.

16.   Blend again, until the whole mess achieves a consistency where you think you might be able to suck it up through a straw.

17.   Try to ignore fact that it has gone from beautiful beef, avocado and bacon burgers to seriously ugly blender full of sludge.

18.   Tip sludge formerly known as beef, avocado and bacon burgers into glass.

19. Pop straw into sludge.

20. Look at sludge in glass and hope it tastes like the meaty goodness that it once was; visualise beef, avocado and bacon burgers in original state, try to hold into that image as . . .

21. Raise glass to lips.

22. Suck on straw for all you are worth, expecting a mouthful of meaty goodness to follow.

23. Stop sucking, as you realise this is not taste of meaty goodness, but mouthful of horrible-tasting sludge.

24. Marvel at how something that was, just a few seconds earlier, one of the great taste sensations of the world has miraculously and horribly become inedible gunk. How is this possible?

25. Forget burger soup idea and dispose of the whole nightmarish failed experiment down sink.

26. Watch TV in attempt to shut out meat cravings.

BEST MEAL EVER?

A meat-lover's pizza.

WORST MEAL EVER?

Burgers in a blender.

THE TRUTH ABOUT DAN CARTER'S UNDIES

Dan Carter has been a mate and a team-mate for many years now. I think he's the best first five-eighth in world rugby.

But there is a dark side to Mr Carter that I feel is my duty to bring to the attention of the book-reading public; an evil streak within the man that comes to the fore at the worst possible moment. Only now can the truth about his underpants be revealed. This is a

THE PALACE

secret
t and
hing
with
Dan
ngs

Dear Mr Williams,

My loyal subjects at MI6 inform me that you are writing a book of anecdotes, due to be published later this year. They also tell me that in this publication you allude to a 'date' involving yourself and myself.

I must inform you that the Crown would take a very dim view of any suggestion that we, and yourself, in any way 'hooked up' — or whatever it is you young people call this sort of thing these days. As far as I am concerned our meetings have been strictly of a formal, business nature, as part of the day-to-day duties of the Reigning Monarch. If you have taken a different view of things, that is very much up to you.

Just to set the record straight, Mr Williams, things would never have worked out between us. Not only am I Queen, but I am also a married woman, not given to extra-marital affairs (unlike some members of my family). Also our differences in age, height and class would have proved insurmountable.

I hope you will use the opportunity of your book to put matters straight. Should you choose not to, I have my lawyers looking into the constitutional powers of the Monarchy today, when it comes to treason and beheading those subjects who diplease them.

Other than that, best of luck with the book.

Regards,

The Queen

P.S. We made the semi-finals of the 2007 World Cup and you didn't — ha ha!

ocking I know, and I'm
sure everyone will look at Dan in a whole new
light now — but I felt the public had a right to know the truth.

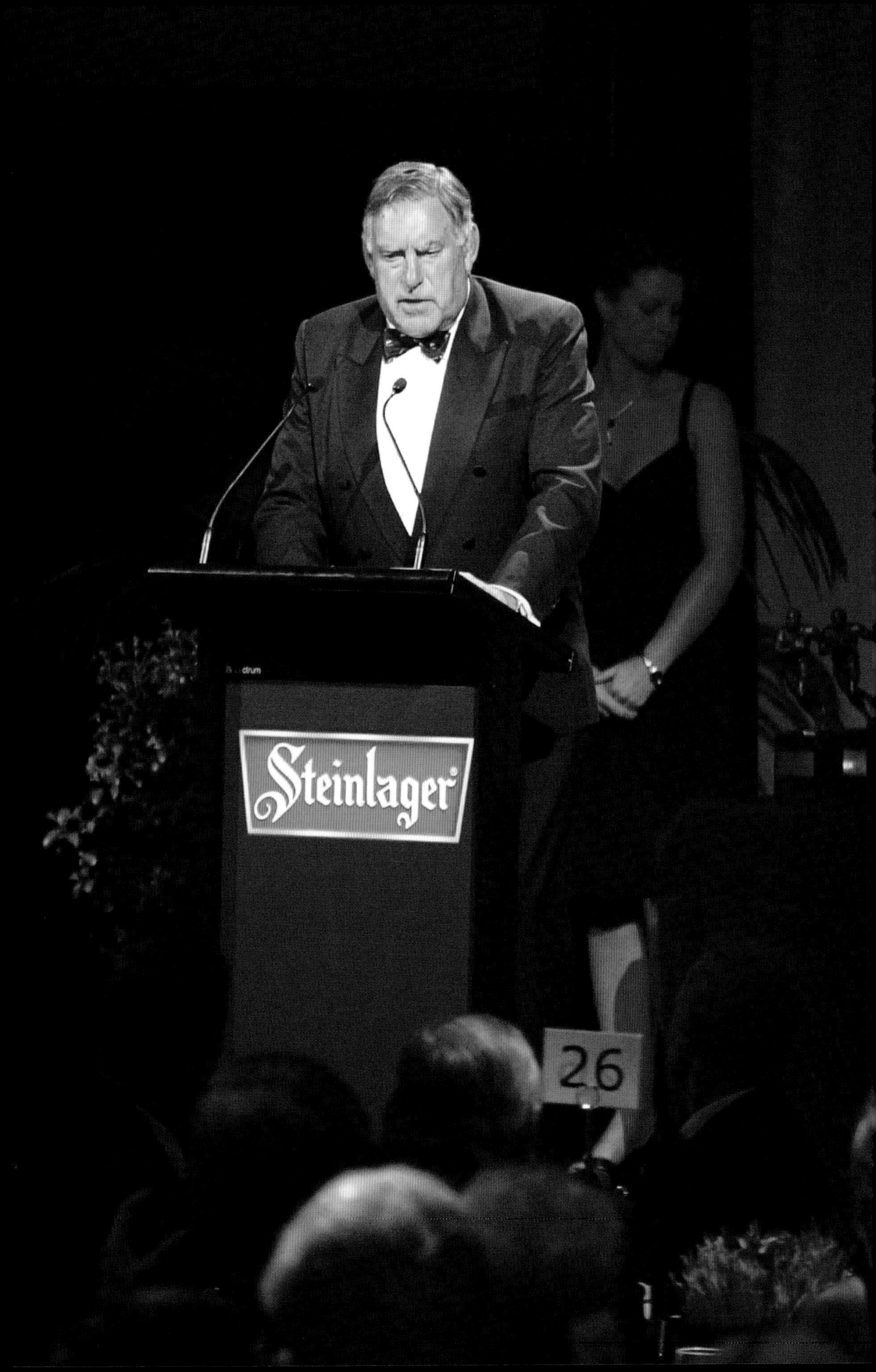
Steinlager
26

BLOKES TODAY ARE NOT SOFT

I reckon there used to be this idea of the true Kiwi bloke that everyone could relate to: the farmer; the classic Kiwi farmer — the Colin Meads type. But that doesn't work these days, when most of us don't live in places actually surrounded by grass. Hell, where I live you can cut the lawn with a pair of scissors. Actually, once I did try to cut the lawn at my Mum's place with a pair of scissors, but that's probably a story for another time.

And I guess in the eyes of some people it means that we've all gone soft. I don't buy that, because all that's happening is the times are changing. If you look at Colin Meads these days, even he's having

Okay, they might all be listening to Colin Meads, but I bet he's not the one they're looking at.

to move with the times like the rest of us. He's doing the corporate dinners and the corporate lunches and he's making a buck out of it. He's taking himself into a world that isn't where he'd naturally be 'himself', and he's turned his yarns, the pub yarns he'd tell his mates, into a business. And good on him for that.

He hasn't gone soft; he's still bloody Colin Meads, isn't he?

So the reality is just that because most guys, these days, grow up in cities it doesn't mean we've all gone soft. Just because I'm from Auckland doesn't mean I'm a Jaffa — hard on the outside, but soft in the middle. (I'm also not 'just another fuckwit from Auckland', thank you very much.) You measure how soft a bloke is not by where he's from and/or if vast swathes of green grass surround him when he's there; you measure it by what he does. That's the bottom line as far as I'm concerned. End of bloody story.

BEST SPORTSMAN OF ALL TIME?

Geoff Thomas. Never fails to go home without winning something, catching something or killing something.

FUN WITH JOURNALISTS

I guess I've got what you'd call a love/hate relationship with the media. Sometimes I guess they love me; sometimes I bet they hate my guts.

The thing is my whole rugby career, because I started playing so late, has pretty much always been in the media. I started late and moved through to the top echelon quite quickly so, I guess, as a bit of a bolter, I became of interest to them. But the thing is, as I was growing as a rugby player, I was also growing up as a human to, I guess, the point where I'm as grown up as I'll ever be. Okay, I'm sure there are plenty who would say this still isn't as grown up as it should be, but we won't go down that road here.

What I'm getting at is how what they'd write and say about me used to really frustrate me, because it was at a time when I was still getting used to who I am, as well as being this rugby player who didn't quite fit the mould of what rugby players in this country should be like. They were publicly charting the highs and lows of my whole life, not just the game I happen to be playing.

And then, as I got older, they started commenting more and more on my life outside rugby; started to say things that affected my family, my friends and my relationships. But the people making these comments, and the things they were saying, they weren't actually there, or they didn't get it from the source. So to me that can't be the truth, or even actually real. Or, at best, it's a glossed-over version of what is real. At worst, they were so outrageously wrong — or telling flat-out lies.

It took me a long time to get my head round that; to get to the point where I didn't care what they wrote because so little of it was real. And then it took me a while longer to figure out the game they're playing — like ringing you up to get a quote about a team-mate, about something you know is a bullshit rumour, because if they can get the quote it makes it a rumour worth printing and whether it is true or not doesn't really mean a thing, in the grand sweep of things.

Okay, I confess, I'm still not over this side of dealing with the media. If a journalist turns up at my door unannounced (as they have been known to) looking for a story, I'll tell them in no uncertain terms to piss off. Because there are times and there are places where journalists can talk to me and turning up on my doorstep is not one of them. Mind you, within the structures that are set up to give the media access to mugs like me who run around a footie paddock for a living, there is plenty of scope to have a bit of fun.

In the run-up to the 2003 World Cup I broke a bone in my foot, the sort of injury you find more with soccer players than rugby players. Of course all I wanted to do was to get running again, as soon as possible, so they whacked me in this moonboot thing, so I could keep on moving, and carry on with weight training and the like. It was a stylish-looking thing and at a press conference

'Okay, how can I put this so you'll understand? How about: if you don't get these things out of my face I will belt someone — is that clear enough?'

someone from the press eventually asked me about it.

Sensing an opportunity for a bit of fun, I started feeding them all this nonsense about how it was this new hi-tech thing that adidas had designed especially for me — as a prototype. And they started taking me seriously, asking me all these questions about how much money adidas were spending on the project and stuff like that. I'm sure there were a fair number of journos there going 'What is this dickhead on about? It's a bloody standard medical moonboot,' but the fact that some of them were scribbling down whatever I was rabbiting on about was utterly worth any grief I got later.

Like I was saying: love/hate. Other than that, me and the media, well, we get along just fine.

One of the men in this photo is telling a big fat lie. The rest are writing it down.

HOW TO TAKE IT
LIKE A MAN

It's a contact sport and sometimes during a contact sport shit happens that ends with you getting in the shit, and this chapter is all about that shit and how you get into it — and how you face up to it.

A lot of guys we play try to wind me up 'cause I guess they think that because of the way I am and the way I play, I'll snap. And when I was first starting out, quite often they'd be right. And if I didn't actually snap and get binned, I'd at least do something stupid and give away penalties. Which is kinda the whole point of the game and the shit that goes on under the surface during a game. You do stuff like that, target a guy because you know he's volatile — and there's generally one in every team who is — and you keep winding him up and hopefully he'll snap and do something mental. I think they call it sportsmanship; trying to get that little edge any way you can.

David Giffin. Yeah, he got the ball — but we got the points.

Having said all that, there's not a lot of what you'd call sledging in rugby, certainly not in the way cricketers can stand around all day yapping at each other. Mostly you're too busy running around the paddock to worry about giving another bloke any lip. About as exciting as it gets is when you're standing in the lineout and the opportunity arises to give someone a hard time — usually the opposing lineout caller, daring him to call himself because all the cameras are on him. I remember, back in 2003, against the Wallabies, I think it was in Sydney, and David Giffin had a crack at me as we're forming up for a lineout. 'Hey, Williams,' he goes, 'they brought you into this fucking team to win lineouts, mate. You haven't won any, so what the hell are you doing here?' Luckily, we were up by 40 points or something so I could turn back to him and go, 'Yeah, good point, spot on the money there, buddy, but I am still here and luckily I've got seven backs behind me who can still kick your arse without me. So do you want this lineout ball, or can I have one?'

It probably sounds weird in a game as physical as rugby, but a lot of the people you play against are your mates, in the sense that you see them so bloody often and you end up having beers with them so often after the games, that you're more likely to be running round talking about how you had too many beers the previous weekend then having a laugh and trying to beat each other to the ball, rather than trying to beat the shit out of each other. Like when I do the haka, quite often the bloke opposite me, who I'm trying to psych out with my take-no-prisoners stare, is trying not to crack up, rather than shaking in his boots. After the game they'll come up to me and says stuff like 'Jeez, what were you doing, man? You lost the plot there.' And when I point out that I had the spirit in me and I was trying to stare them down, they say things like, 'But I couldn't look at you, man, not without cracking up.' Not exactly the sort of fear the haka is meant to inspire in the opposition, I'm afraid.

Which is not to say that just because you're matey with a bloke off the field and you'll share a beer with him after a game, that when you're up against him on the field you're going to hold back when it comes to throwing the kitchen sink at him. The point of the game, after all, is to play as hard as you can for as long as you can.

And if you can get away with taking a shot at him along the way, then you're going to take that chance.

Like the big, hairy French caveman monster who broke my jaw; some people have suggested to me that he raised his elbow, came up into the tackle on purpose. Now I don't believe that; I think it was one of those things that happened. I wasn't grumpy about it then, and me and him had a yarn about it a couple of years later and all was cool. But that won't stop me giving it a little extra if we happen to meet on the field again, and I get the chance to get a good shot on him. And I'm sure he knows that, because that sort of thing — the little paybacks — is all part and parcel of the game.

Which is not to say that I'm going to take a swing at him, because, quite frankly, these days punching someone's lights out on the field isn't so much a thing of legend as something a mug who's lost his cool will do.

Because the thing about taking a swing at someone on the field is that even though there are times you really want to, and sometimes you'll have the arm cocked, ready to let fly, you've got to keep it in your head.

There'll be consequences if you take the shot.

Sure, you might smack him there and then and it might sort something out at that moment, but the way the game is now, chances are you won't be round for your team the next week or the week after that or for several weeks after that if you clock him real good. And several weeks is most of a Super 14 or a Super 12 or a Super whatever number it is this year, and that's time when you should be impressing the AB selectors and instead you're sitting in the stands.

Eyes closed as he considers the consequences of taking the shot.
(Note impressive second place facial hair.)

126

And if you're in the ABs, playing Australia or South Africa in the Tri-Nations, say, and you punch someone, the chances are you'll be playing the same team in a week or two and if the guy you whacked is out there playing while you're sitting in the stands, suspended, who's the winner then? Add to that the fact that because the teams are always sitting down and having a quiet beer together after the game, that the bloke who played that week, while you were in the stands, in your number ones, watching, will probably be there giving you a hard time about how things turned out. It's just not worth the grief, to be honest. Sure, it's hard to keep all that in your head when you're fired up and want to dish out some instant justice, there and then, but you have to try and rein it in, if you want to play.

'Hey Al, tell your mum thanks for the biscuits.'

At the end of the day, whatever happens on the field, no matter how malicious it is, it has to stay on the field — at least where the players are concerned. And that means keeping your cool and winning the game, rather than decking anyone. That's the best payback there is. You expect that shit will happen on the field — that you'll get caught in the wrong place and someone will take a shot when they think they can get away with it (and, yes, we all do it and we all expect it to happen to us) — so the best way of dealing with it is by looking at the scoreboard at the end of the game and seeing you're the ones in front.

Of course, with so many cameras and so many officials these days, there's a fair chunk of stuff that ends up being dealt with off the field, and with a trip to the judiciary.

And, yeah, I've had my fair share of these; of being forced to front up and take my punishment like a man.

My most famous — or infamous, I guess — trip to the judiciary was back in the 2005 Super 12, when I copped six weeks for trampling Richie McCaw's head, towards the end of the 41–19 monstering we were getting by the Crusaders at Eden Park. Not a good night all round. Richie and I are good mates now — I mean, he let me stay at his place rent free for a season, so things can't be too bad between us, eh? And we've talked about what happened

A picture of innocence.

that night, and the current version we're happy to agree on is that he was doing his work, doing what Richie does better than anyone else in the world, getting the ball. Then he fell over, on our side of things, and a bunch of us piled in. And, yeah, I got his neck and then moved round to ruck his back, but as to deliberately going for his head — he doesn't believe I did that. So we're cool with that and that is where it rests between us.

But of course something like that never ever rests just between the players involved — not at the time it happens — because there's a whole judicial process that kicks into gear pretty much from the second your boot makes contact with his head. And how it works goes something like this: you get cited, someone comes up to you with the news, after the game — even though you've probably figured it out long before that — like just after Paddy O'Brien has waved a red card in your face and you're walking back towards the sheds.

Once you've been cited, you basically become best friends with your team's analysis man, as you go over and over the available TV footage, trying to find the one angle that makes everything look less like an act of thuggery and more like a clumsy mistake. With the ABs, Steve Hansen is the man you want on your side here because not only is he the great analysis man, he is also never ever wrong and everyone who knows him knows that.

On Monday or Tuesday you'll get notified where and when you'll need to front the judiciary and face your music. This is probably the least favourite reason of all to get dressed up in the number ones, which leaves you both pissed off and nervous when you and your legal representative walk in for your hearing.

The hearings themselves are pretty nerve-wracking, as you sit there in front of this jury, listening to the referee's report and looking at the incident over and over again.

The way everything comes down to that one moment and how nothing that has happened in the game up until then means anything. So you sit there having all these discussions about the tiniest things: which way your eyes are looking as you're rucking the guy; and how it looks different on this angle than on the other angle . . .

But, at the end of the day, basically you're at the mercy of whoever it is on the jury: if they're sticklers for the laws, there to defend the decision of the officials; or if they've got a bee in their bonnet about cleaning up the game; or, if it's your lucky day, if they are willing to look at the wider picture. There was one time I was up for smacking someone and the head jury guy was really cool about it, saying, 'He's holding your jersey, you're frustrated, I don't see the issue here.' Sweet, but not how it usually pans out.

You can speak in your own defence, but a lot of the guys choose

131

not to. Among the excuses unlikely to fly at a judicial hearing, I imagine, would be:

'I know it *looks* like I'm rucking his head, Your Honour, but if you look carefully at the tape you'll see he's actually head-butting my foot. If anyone should be up on a charge it's him!'

'Three weeks? I almost broke my freakin' finger punching that bastard — why isn't that punishment enough? And he bloody deserved it too.'

'I have size 14 feet and they're a long way from my brain — sometimes the message about where or where not to stand doesn't get through in time. It's simple physiology, really.'

'But he's French! I consider it payback for what the bastards did to Buck Shelford's testicle in Nantes back in 1986.'

'I'm a lock; he's a halfback — where else am I going to tackle him except round the neck? If I had to bend any lower I'd put my back out!'

'He's a prop, M'lord! A smack across the chops is the only language they understand!'

'But if you play the tape backwards, Your Majesty, you'll see what I'm really doing is I'm taking my foot *off* his head — repeatedly.'

'This is a joke, right? I mean, since when has punching an Australian been a crime?'

Then, after all is said and done and everything's been watched over and over and over again, they send you out while they decide, then you get called back in and if they find you guilty you start talking all over again about how long the punishment should be. One week: I'm good with that. Two weeks: not so good. Six weeks: shit, that definitely didn't go so well.

All in all, not a process you want to go through if you can help it. Hell, I miss enough games through injury without adding stupidity into the mix.

IT'S OKAY TO LIE, AS LONG AS YOU LIE WELL

When you're a kid you get it drummed into you that lying is a bad thing. For the most part that's probably a fair call because fronting up and owning up is the honourable way of doing things and no one likes someone who bullshits their way through life.

But there are times and places when I reckon a good lie can absolutely be the way to go — especially if it's all in the name of good clean fun.

Dan Carter and I are terrible liars, especially when we're overseas, where we're less likely to get recognised. If we're in, say, a shop and the old 'Where are you from and what do you do?' conversation starts up, we're fairly adept at spinning a line of crap that'll keep things going for a while. Being bow-tie salesmen, from New Zealand, for example, is a good conversation starter in any European nation.

Okay, sure they're probably thinking 'Who are these idiot New Zealanders? Everyone in the world knows New Zealanders know nothing about ties, let alone bow ties,' but that's not the point here. The point is it is a total lie and no one is getting hurt and there is nothing wrong with that.

One of my personal faves was in Cardiff, when we'd flown in from, I think, Rome and our luggage hadn't turned up (yes, it happens to the All Blacks too and believe me when I say losing the ABs' luggage is an impressive amount of luggage to lose). So Dan and I are still in our travel tracksuits when we wander into a pub for a couple of quiet ones.

While we're sipping our beers we get talking to some of the locals, who are wondering who these track-suited blokes are in their pub.

So we tell them we're dolphin trainers, from New Zealand. For a good hour (and a few beers) we manage to spin the line about how they're going to build this aquarium in Cardiff and that we're here from a similar sort of place, down in New Zealand, where we have these trained dolphins who do all these tricks, to start training the dolphins for the new Cardiff aquarium or marine-land or whatever they call a place where you go to watch dolphins do tricks when you're in Wales. And I swear we had them going and if it hadn't been for the bunch of students who walked in and recognised us, we would have walked out of that bar with our cover intact and

One of these men is standing on a box.

there'd be a bunch of people in Cardiff wondering, to this day, whatever happened to the place they were meant to build, with the performing dolphins.

There is absolutely nothing wrong with a good lie, as long as no one (especially not the dolphins) is getting hurt in the process and it's all in the name of good, clean fun (and relieving the tedium when you're on tour). And children, don't let your parents convince you otherwise.

THE GLAMOROUS LIFE OF AN ALL BLACK

Playing for the All Blacks; travelling the world, playing the sport you love; making a good living doing it. Every kid's dream, eh?

Yeah, it's great, it's the best job and the best thing in the world for me, but that doesn't mean you shouldn't acknowledge the fact that it is a job and like any job it can get boring at times. I think it's only fair to talk about that stuff as well.

Like, if you're on tour with the All Blacks, you're usually playing on Saturdays, which means the rest of the week, on tour, usually breaks down something like this:

Do as I say, not as I do.

Sunday: Travel day/every bit of your body hurts day — commonly called 'recovery'. So when you're recovering you're actually packing up your stuff and getting it on a bus or a plane. At least I can sleep on buses or planes, which is a good thing at any time but especially when you're meant to be 'recovering'. Basically, by the end of Sunday you're in another town or another country or on a plane heading towards another country and, depending on how far you're flying and whether the international date line comes into play, it might be back to being Saturday again, or you might have skipped Sunday and gone straight to Monday. Sunday can be pretty confusing at times, is all I'm saying here.

Luggage boy — about my status in life.

Monday: Training in the morning, then a weights session in the afternoon. And the rest of the day gets chewed up with team meetings and debrief sessions and so forth. It's not uncommon for me and Shag (Steve Hansen) to still be up at 10 o'clock going through the playback of how and why we managed to cock up a particular lineout and whether or not it was my fault.

Tuesday: Like Monday, with training in the morning, except that the afternoon weights session is optional.

> If Shag and I are still going over the lineouts then we must have really cocked them up on Saturday.

Wednesday: Like Monday and Tuesday, with training in the morning, and the afternoon weights session is optional.

Which is not to say that Tuesday and Wednesday are easy half-days. Tuesday and Wednesday are when all the other stuff comes into play: the promotional events you need to attend (and which can mean dressing up in the dreaded number ones); the media sessions; shooting any stuff the TV people might need for the TV coverage; in other words, all the stuff that comes with the territory when you're part of the All Blacks road show. It's not that I'm saying that all this stuff isn't worthwhile, or isn't fun at times, but you don't get much of a chance on these days to get out and about, actually check out whatever part of the planet you happen to be on.

Thursday: Training in the morning, the afternoons are generally pretty free, giving the boys the opportunity to get out and do something they want — golf or whatever. I'm not a big golfer and golf isn't the thing it was back in the days of Justin Marshall, Mehrts, Carlos and all those boys, but you still get the occasional hacker like Jimmy Cowan who considers himself to be pretty good and will try to take the money off anyone willing to have a go.

Actually, taking money off each other is quite a big thing when you're on tour — or at any time really, when you're with a bunch of rugby players trying to keep things interesting. Thursday, when you're with the team, is lunch money day, the day the manager

Andy Ellis and me — Rule 1: always pick on the little guys.

140

gives us 50 bucks each to cover lunch and dinner for the meals where we have to fend for ourselves. So he'll be handing out the cash and then what'll happen is someone, let's say Ma'a Nonu, will hold up The Rock (as in 'rock, paper, scissors') to me and I'll be like 'Hell yeah, I'm in' and we'll 'Rock Off' for the 50 bucks. Rock, paper, scissors; winner takes all. A lot of the time it's the back-seat-of-the-bus guys who start things. On the 2008 end-of-year tour it was Anthony Boric who kept getting called out — yeah, we all took a fair bit of money off Anthony Boric that tour. And it's not small change either, if you get on a roll and clean out half a dozen guys, you're walking off that bus with $300 — which buys a lot of lunch.

Friday: Apart from a captain's run, this is the easiest of all the touring days, so you can get out a bit, relax before tomorrow's game. Sometimes it's really simple, like going to the movies or going shopping, depending on where in the world you are. If you're in Europe it's pretty good because a group of you — you always go out in groups — can wander around and you don't get recognised so much, or hassled so much. There are other things that go on, like there are a few guys who like to go out for a shoot whenever they can — clay pigeons, not seals, just for the record.

Then there are the things that get organised for us, either by the sponsors or by the entertainment committee. In Scotland, one year, we watched pig racing, which was a blast. And in Ireland there was the dog racing and yet another chance for the boys to take money off each other.

The dog racing — mainly because no one has the foggiest idea what makes a good dog and what's a bad dog — works along the lines that the team divides up into betting syndicates. Everyone throws their money into a syndicate betting pool and together you make your picks for the five or six races we're there for. Then, at the end of the evening, the syndicate which has won the most money takes the lot, everyone's winnings. So you'll get this range of strategies

Richie fires at will.

going on across the evening; strategies that reveal a lot about the true nature of the boys involved. At one end of the spectrum you have your cowboys who go hard from race one, trying to build up a lead. Then you've got your more conservative punters who pretend they know what they're doing (even though they have no friggin' clue) and who make what they reckon are careful, considered bets. And then you have Steve Hansen. Shag is one of those guys who doesn't give away anything, so he plays it all pretty hard. By the end of the night you've got a couple of syndicates vying for the win, giving each other heaps. At the other end of proceedings there'll be syndicates who are so far behind they're throwing what money they've got left on the worst mongrel in the field, trying either to stage a miracle come-back or to lose everything so the pack of bastards who do win don't end up pocketing any of their cash. All in all, a good night out for the boys.

But the truth of the matter is most of touring with the ABs boils down to travelling, training and hotel rooms.

Lots and lots of time in hotels rooms: chilling out, watching TV, feeling tired and sore. And Texas Hold'em; the boys play masses and masses of Texas Hold'em, to keep the boredom at bay until . . .

Saturday: Match day; what it's all about. Forget everything else; this is why we're here. Pulling on that black shirt is still the best feeling any kid can have, even when he's a grown up one like me.

OKAY, I CONFESS, THERE ARE PERKS TOO

It'd be wrong of me to bang on about the downsides of being an All Black — the lack of privacy, all the boring bits and so forth — without acknowledging that there is plenty of stuff that is shit hot about doing what I do for a living, about being in the position I'm in. Because of the mana the All Black jersey has, there are normally plenty of sponsors who look after you, with free stuff and taking you out and taking you to places you wouldn't normally get to go to. Let's be honest here, it doesn't matter who you are or what you do, it is a basic human fact of life: free stuff is the bomb.

When you're an All Black, there are also, obviously, flow-on effects in that people want to pay you to do a marketing campaign; and that the power of the jersey means that any business you're involved in automatically gets more of a profile, simply because you're involved. It's not everything, but in business you take every advantage you can get. And as long as you're not stupid about it, and be very clear about what it is you're selling and why you're selling it (correct answer = not just for the money), then I don't see anything wrong with this side of the modern game. It's a global sport and the All Blacks are the #1 brand, and I have a limited window of opportunity in terms of playing time, therefore I'd be a mug not to use that time wisely.

Then there are your more basic, day-to-day perks, like people buying you beers when you're out. One of the great things about New Zealand, I reckon, is that people are mainly positive about things, so you get more comments along the line of 'Good game, mate' or 'Bad luck, mate' if you've lost, than you get the finger pointers and the smart-arse comments. Sure, sometimes complete strangers want to talk to you when you're not in the mood, but for the most part people are pretty respectful and if they do happen to get onto the whole 'You know what's wrong with rugby these days?' roll it's because New Zealanders are passionate about their rugby, which means they feel connected with what I do, so I don't have any problem with that at all. Say what you think, man. Better than keeping it in — just don't expect me to stand here all night listening to you and we'll get on fine.

Sometimes the perk will come in the form of doing something totally unexpected, as a team, just because needs must. Like there was a time in Paris when, for some reason, probably to get us to the game on time, the team bus drove the wrong way up the Champs-

Age before beauty.

Élysées. We had a police escort leading us head on into a horde of Frenchies who all drive like mad things at the best of times, let alone when there are all these flashing lights and a bloody great bus coming the wrong way at you. That was pretty off the hook and kinda cool; so I'd class that as a definite perk because no way would I try that on my own, in a rented car, instead of being on the All Black bus.

Occasionally, very occasionally, you get the complete bonus, get-out-of-jail-free perk.

For example, you might have happened to be running a bit late for training and gone through an orange light and when the cop pulls you over he susses who you are and after a bit of a chat he lets you off with a warning instead of a fine. Not that I'm saying this has ever happened to me. Also I'm pretty sure that sort of thing cuts both ways. I don't imagine if I was pulled over for speeding, say, while driving through Hamilton on my way to Raglan, and the cop was a Chiefs fan, that anyone would be getting off anything — and I'd probably get a lecture on why I, personally, cost us the World Cup in 2003 thrown in along with the ticket.

But I'd be lying if I didn't say that wearing the silver fern on your chest doesn't have its perks, and that the perks far outweigh the downsides. Especially the free stuff, man. Free stuff is the best and more people should have more access to free stuff — especially if they are writers who collaborate on books with All Blacks, or so I'm told.

ON GOING OUT

Sometimes I wish I was a halfback. Not actually on the field, but when I'm going out on the town. Halfbacks aren't two metres tall, so they blend in and look innocent — even when they're not being innocent. No one sees them. And then, when the trouble starts, they're off like a flash.

I admit, sometimes when I walk into a place, I'll slouch — crouch down, just a bit. I just want to get through the crowd, get to where I'm going, sit down and have dinner or whatever, without feeling that people are looking at me and who I'm with and saying stuff along the lines of: 'Are they having fun?' 'What the hell is he wearing?' All that kind of stuff; I mean, like it's important to anyone but me and who I'm with what I happen to be wearing or if I'm smiling at that particular time? Really, who gives a toss? Maybe I just had a real shit time trying to find a carpark, and that's why I'm not smiling.

But apparently some people must actually give a toss; otherwise it wouldn't end up in the gossip pages on Sunday would it?

Casey is way hotter than me.

Seriously, why is it news if I pop down to my nearest bar for a quiet drink with Richie, and our girlfriends are with us? But it must be because I read about it in the paper one Sunday. It's like the start of a bad joke: two All Blacks walk into a bar, and then shit happens. Or not. Nothing happened, it was a quiet night out. Yet it ends up in the paper; and usually in a way that is catty and stupid. It's certainly one of the things that hacks me off about Auckland — because Auckland is about the only place it happens — and, quite frankly, I wish they'd give it a rest.

Which isn't to say that I'll shy away from going out. Hell no, I like going out; I'm not going to hide all the time, staying home playing video games, dressed as Spiderman. The hermit lifestyle, you'll be surprised to learn, is really not my thing. All I have to master now is not getting into strife when I do go out.

This brings me back to the fact that halfbacks, I reckon, have it way easier when it comes to going out and avoiding trouble; because they're lower to the ground and they can escape unnoticed. And that's all I'm saying on the matter — for now.

SPIDERMAN AND ME

It's one of those things that really divides people. It's even worse than whether you're from Auckland or not from Auckland, as to how people look at you. It divides the nation, I reckon.

Me? I am firmly in favour of dressing up. By that I don't mean putting on the number ones and heading out (although, if that's what spins your wheels, all respect to you for that). What I mean is dressing up, as in what you might call 'fancy dress' — getting totally out of your comfort zone and turning yourself into something/someone you totally are not.

I know there are a lot of people who just don't get the whole dressing up thing (one of them is the rooster I'm writing this book with) but I reckon it's got a heck of a lot going for it. For starters, if you get a bunch of people together in a room and everyone is dressed up in some stupid costume, just for the hell of it, suddenly everyone's on a level playing field. It doesn't matter who you are or what you do outside that room; inside the room you're whoever/whatever you're dressed as and the ice is well and truly broken, so you're away laughing.

My personal costume of choice, obviously, is Spiderman. I like that Peter Parker doesn't have too much of a ridiculous superpower. He's just this ordinary guy who happened to get bitten by a radioactive spider which meant he could do cool shit, like getting across town real quick. Try driving round Auckland for any length of time and you'll soon wish you were Spiderman too.

This is the story of how the Spiderman/dressing up thing started. As with a lot of the stories in my life over the last few years — most of which I am not at liberty to divulge — it involves a certain sly dog by the name of Dan Carter. Often, when I'm the big lug getting in all the trouble, there'll be this little kid, the one who was egging me on to start with, slipping out the door, unnoticed. That, my friends, is Daniel Carter in a nutshell.

It was at the end of a campaign and we were in Auckland, still staying in the hotel. It'd been a long night, but we were still ready to crack on come the next morning. This is when the idea of dressing up came up and once that was seized upon as the way to go for the day a quick phone-call went out to brother Jay to come and pick us up, take us somewhere where we can find costumes for Dan and me to dress up in.

And so, with young bro' as chauffeur, we shot off to First Scene, where the staff got to watch for a while on a nice quiet morning two idiots charging round the place, trying on every superhero costume we could get our hands on, until we settled on the two that seemed to sum up our respective personalities: Spiderman and The Phantom. Thus attired, we thanked the lovely people for their help, paid our money, and set out to save the city.

Actually, what the city probably needed saving from was us, as we spent the rest of the day being driven round by Jay, daring each other to use our superpowers for good, not evil; mainly by going into bars in our costumes. Of course, this being Auckland and him being Dan Carter, we ended up at a model agency, trying to get them to sign us (Spiderman and The Phantom, not Ali and Dan) on as models. In reality we were booked to go to some Fashion Week show that night and we wanted to go dressed up in our costumes. For some reason this wasn't going down so well. We haven't got any other clothes with us, we pointed out. This didn't fly either, and more fashionably appropriate clothing was rounded up for us. But we did, I'm proud to say, manage to take our masks with us, which we kept on as often as possible, in order to mask our true identities.

Crime-fighting superhero? Or just a big idiot? You be the judge.

Spiderman still makes fairly regular appearances in my life — when there are things that need retrieving from up trees, or things that need to be said that only a superhero can say, for example. Probably the most widely known of Spidey's appearances was a certain press session when I was with the Crusaders. Again the hand of Mr Carter was behind that one. It started with a bet, that I wouldn't do my press call dressed as Spiderman. Three hundred bucks, I think I got him up to. I consider it some of the easiest money I've ever taken off Mr Carter.

And so it came to pass that after training one day, when it was my turn to front up and answer the usual round of questions, that Spiderman turned up instead.

And it worked a treat. Anyone who ever watches sports press conferences on TV will know that, for the most part, they're pretty dull, with the players or coaches giving the same by-the-book, non-committal answer to the same set of by-the-book questions. It's a whole exercise in not saying very much and I pretty much hate doing them. But, suddenly, when Spiderman turns up instead of this Williams bloke, there are a whole heap of new and more interesting questions for the journos to ask: like what the hell is Spiderman doing here? Not only did this play totally into my hands — in that they were asking me all this stuff about Spidey rather than the usual crap — but I think they got into it as well.

But it's one thing turning up to a press conference dressed as a superhero, it's another thing to make an exit worthy of the appearance — i.e. before you start making more of a dork of yourself than you already are — which is where Ross Filipo came into it. Dan was out injured, so Ross was brought into play to don the Phantom costume and, at precisely the right moment, which was just before I started making too much of an idiot of myself in front of the cameras, to run up to Spidey and inform him that we were needed, in true superhero fashion, 'back in town'. Full credit to Floss for performing his super-duties superbly and, most importantly, on time; and it was a quiet tap on the shoulder from The Ghost Who Walks, and Spiderman and The Phantom made good their escape back to the dressing rooms.

Of course, after the event, there were some rumblings among the management that I hadn't adequately fulfilled my media responsibilities, but when Robbie Deans saw the funny side of it, everything was sweet. I can certainly think of other coaches who would have lost their lid if I pulled a stunt like that on their watch.

Spiderman: making the world safe for idiots everywhere. And who knows where and when he will pop up next.

DIRTIEST, CHEATINGEST TEAM I'VE EVER PLAYED AGAINST?

My brother, backyard cricket.

DOING IT FOR THE KIDS

Yeah, it's probably one of the biggest clichés in sport, but one of the coolest things about the job I do is the fact that kids look up to you. Having a bunch of kids hanging out, waiting to get your autograph is actually pretty neat — and it works both ways, I reckon: they feel good getting the autograph, and it pumps you up a bit too. It's always nice to feel wanted.

Signing autographs for a bunch of kids can go any number of ways. Most of the time everyone's nice and polite and it'll be, 'Excuse me, can I have your autograph please?' Then you get the kids who tell it more like it is: 'Hey, you, the tall guy! Give me your autograph!' But that's cool, that's all part of the fun. Then there're the kids who push it even further: 'Hey, come over here and give me your bloody autograph!' Which is pushing it a bit far and generally gets

Jimmy Cowan scratches his head. Come on mate, it's your name! It's not that hard to remember!

155

the evil eye and a 'Nah, you come over here,' if they're lucky. And then you get the kids who come up and ask you for your autograph even though they don't actually want your autograph, but they've been pimped out by their parents, so when you start talking to them they tell you, 'Nah, I don't actually know who you are, but my mum wants it — she's over there.'

It's the honesty of kids that is the best thing about them. They just say what they think and what they want to say. A lot like me, I guess. Maybe I just forgot to grow up.

Like Santa, but without the beard and red suit.

Once, through a mate of mine I ended up at a kid's birthday party, down at Bayfield, in Herne Bay, my old primary school. And we're playing a game of footy; the kids and their dads and the ring-ins like me, just for a laugh, and my team had just scored a try and we're retreating for the kick-off when this kid comes up to me . . .

'My dad thinks you're shit,' says the kid.

And I'm, like, 'Sorry? Who thinks I'm what?'

'My dad,' says the kid. 'He doesn't think you're very good.'

'Well, who's your dad?' I ask.

And the kid points at this guy on the other team — who has just tuned into the conversation and is freaking out, clearly having visions of me walking all over him the next time me, him and the ball come anywhere near each other.

'Oh, yeah?' I go, letting him sweat for a few seconds before revealing the true nature of my good-natured self. 'Well that's the beauty of life, son. Everyone has their own opinions.'

The kid takes in the depth of my philosophy for about a second before adding, 'But don't worry. He thinks Sione Lauaki's even worse than you.'

I think it's the fact that kids are so straight up, that everything is on the level with them, which got me and Doug Howlett involved in KidsCan. I think if you're out there, using what you've been given — in terms of a life and a career — to help kids, then you're helping a whole bunch of people who still have a chance in life; you're taking the future of this country and directly getting involved in helping them be the most they can. It's a long-term investment.

And it's a direct investment too: shoes, raincoats, food. It's really basic stuff that in New Zealand we can take for granted, but if you drive half an hour south from where I live, it's a whole different world. This is where you give a kid a raincoat and he says, 'Choice, now I can go to school when it rains.' I mean, that sort of thing shouldn't exist in New Zealand, but it does and we want to educate people about what's happening just round the corner. Let's clean up our own backyard before we look elsewhere, eh?

DEALING WITH PREJUDICE
ON THE RUGBY FIELD

One of the great things about playing rugby in New Zealand is the way many, many cultures come together to play our national game. Maori, Samoans, Tongans, Fijians, as well as those who would classify themselves as Pakeha New Zealanders but whose families have come to this great country from many faraway places: Scotland, Ireland, Croatia and so forth.

For all our cultural differences, when we are on that field, dressed in black, we are one simple entity: New Zealand.

But within the game of rugby in this country, there is still one group of people who are discriminated against on an almost daily basis. They are a group sadly maligned and abused not for who they are or what they do or stand for, but simply because of what they are. I talk, of course, of the M'orange — the Men of the Orange.

Paul Tito — The Fish.

159

They go by many other names: gingas, ginger nuts, fire-trucks, orange-atans, Fanta-pants, carrot-tops, blood-nuts, match-sticks . . . No group, on the sporting field, or in life, cops more flak for something that is no fault of their own than the M'orange.

To help to integrate and accept the M'orange into the game of rugby and, by example, into the rest of society, I think there should be a quota system introduced requiring each team to achieve a certain level of ginger-ness before they are allowed to take the field. The way this would work is that each player would be rated on a Ginga Scale of 0 to 5; with the aim being that each team had to achieve a total of 8 Ginga Points (in the starting XV) before they'd get the thumbs up.

A player like James 'Chucky' Ryan would obviously score an automatic five on the Ginga Scale and would, therefore, be a huge asset to any team.

My brother Jay, having inherited, via our proud Scottish ancestry, a distinctly M'orange hue, would also rate a 5. Even better would be The Fish, Paul Tito, whose combination of being extremely pale, with the proud orange hair, plus being Maori, would earn him bonus points, so he'd be at least a 7 if not an 8. Get a Paul Tito in your team and you're sorted on the Ginga Quota.

At the other end of the scale would be your Keven Mealamus and your Rodney So'oialos and your Ma'a Nonus who would struggle to score even a single Ginga Point between them. In fact the only way this could happen would be if Rodney and Ma'a dyed their

160

Chucky and Ali.

dreads ginger as a show of ginga solidarity. This, I reckon, would score them a 2 or even a 3, depending on how it ended up looking.

For most teams the bulk of the required Ginga Points would come by amassing players in your team like Tony Woodcock (a 1, maybe a 2), Andrew Hore (1) and Luke McAlister (1, or 2 if he's got a mo' going on). These are guys for whom the M'orange appears round the fringes — in the sideburns and the facial hair — rather than the full-on bloodnut. I'd put myself in this category, scoring a healthy 2 points when I've got the full growth going; or a 1 when I'm in a more streamlined mode.

There are kinda two interlinked reasons why I think it is important to integrate the M'orange into the game. The first is to integrate them into actual human life as much as possible. These are guys who have grown up dealing with a lot of shit, for no other reason than they have weird-coloured hair. My brother can testify to this. And yes, he'll also testify that it was, on occasions, me giving him the shit. What can I say? It's an easy attack; it's a lazy attack, but when it's your brother you have to use whatever weapon you can, especially when the receiver has little or no defence.

The second reason is that because of this shit, because of the anger that builds up inside the M'orange after a lifetime of abuse, they bring a lot of fire to their game (and not just on top of their heads). They don't really like a lot of people, so when they get on the field they just cut loose in the way only a deeply angry man can.

A Man of the Orange, in full flight, attacking anyone who gets in his way, is a thing to behold.

So the next time you encounter a Man of the Orange, try to remember that even though he looks like a freak, he is a human being just like you, and be nice to him; just in case he snaps and goes ballistic.

FAMILY AND FRIENDS ARE IMPORTANT IN A TIME OF NEED

High on my list of 'Things Never to Do If You Can Absolutely Help It' is breaking your jaw. It is really not a good idea. It hurts like stink and leads to things like living off soup for weeks on end.

But break my jaw I did, when a hairy Frenchman with a head that felt like a cannon-ball smacked into me in Wellington on 9 June 2007.

The second Sebastien Chabal smacked into me, I knew it was broken. I managed to get up pretty quick, but my face wouldn't move the way I wanted it to and when I ran my tongue round the inside of my mouth there was this weird space that wasn't there before. Plus there was blood pissing out everywhere, which is never a good sign.

Now normally I'm a bloke who will give painkillers a swerve if I possibly can, but by the time I got back to the changing room they couldn't get a needle into me quick enough. So, of course, they packed me off to hospital, which is where the fun and games and total disrespect towards me, as a person in pain, started.

The first bit of flak I copped was when the old man rings me at the hospital. Obviously, I'm not that keen on talking on the phone but I think, 'Shit, I better talk to him, he might be worried.' Little did I know he couldn't actually give a rat's arse.

'How are you?'

'I'm a bit fucked, mate. I think it's broken,' I said as best I could, given I could hardly talk.

'Oh, yeah?'

'I think I'll be out for a while. They reckon I won't be able to talk properly for a good six or seven weeks,' I tell him, expecting to get a little sympathy in return.

'Oh, well, that's a blessing,' he says.

'A blessing for who?'

'The nation. To shut you up for six weeks.'

Okay, now I know this was all said in fun – and because I basically started talking at a very young age and never stopped, so Dad could obviously see the irony (and the upside) in me being silenced for a while. And it definitely sums up Dad and me, our relationship: basically we're mates, giving each other a bit of grief. But the point I'm making here is at that particular moment, I wasn't the happiest man on the planet, so getting grief from my old man was not high on the agenda. Oh, the doctors and everyone, they all enjoyed it, they all thought it was a great laugh, but I was, like, 'Well, piss off then,' and end of phone-call. It's all about timing, is what I'm saying – picking your moments to take a dig at your nearest and dearest. Are you getting this now, Dad?

They wired my jaw to make me look like this, honest.

They couldn't operate until the next morning; and I'm waiting there to go in, I'm next in line for theatre, when they come up to me and say that this kid has been brought in, from a car accident or something, and they're asking, 'Ali, do you mind if we put this kid in ahead of you?' And I'm lying there, finding ways to express, through a broken jaw, that of course I don't mind! Why are you even asking me?

After I got out of surgery, they told me it took about three hours to put my jaw back into place. Normally, it takes about an hour and a half. I have to wonder, looking back on it, if possibly my jaw muscles were overdeveloped from all the talking I do and that's what made it such a bloody mission.

The end result for me, of course, was waking up with a mouthful of metal.

Suddenly, I'm back to being a poxy teenager, when I spent two and a half years wearing braces and looking like some kind of freak.

Yeah, special thoughts and a great time of my life to suddenly revisit, with the bonus being that this time everything is wired shut. Brilliant.

I had a good stream of visitors while I was laid up in Hutt Hospital after the operation — Jerry Collins and Piri Weepu and a bunch of others from the AB crew stopped by, which was great — but it's the visit of a couple of other chaps I want to dwell on for a minute here. Let's call them ABC and ABD, so that the names of the guilty parties will remain within the confines of those who need to know.

It was the Monday, I'm pretty sure, and the boys were playing Canada the following weekend so they'd been given the first couple of days of the week off. ABC and ABD had taken full advantage of that mini-break and by the time they rolled in to visit me on Monday afternoon, they were pretty well monstered.

This was all well and good, and all rather amusing, until they realised their ride was gone and decided they'd stay the night with me instead. Now I'm in a room on my own and no way am I having these clowns trying to top and tail with me, so alternative arrangements needed to be made. In the case of ABC, he sorted himself out by taking himself off to the little bathroom in the corner of the room, locking the door and promptly falling asleep on the bog.

Meanwhile, ABD, who is rather popular with the lady-kind, had charmed the nurses into bringing in a La-Z-Boy so he could crash out there. Oh yeah, all the nurses loved having ABD in their ward and were treating him like royalty, tucking him in and making a fuss over his every need. Meanwhile I'm the one with the bloody broken jaw, getting half the love he's getting. How wrong is that? Talk about pouring salt on a man's wounds.

I'm not entirely sure of the precise details — what with the broken jaw and the surgery and the painkillers and everything — but Monday afternoon, while ABC and ABD are in residence at the hospital, was also when Jock Hobbs, the NZRU Chairman, and his wife Nicki dropped in for a visit. Somehow — by good luck or good design or because he's a jammy bastard, I have no idea — ABD wasn't in the room when Jock arrived. Maybe he has a sixth sense about when potentially big trouble is coming, in the form of the boss man who pays our wages, and he'd sensed something and gone off to hide.

Which just left ABC, asleep in the loo, as Jock and Nicki paid their visit. And that bit — that actual visiting bit — was great and it was lovely that they took the time to come and see how I was. Unfortunately, it was also the time ABC decided he needed to have a bit of a spit and this God-awful noise starts coming from the bathroom. And there's me, through my broken jaw, having to lie to the Chairman that the noise is actually coming from the room next door, from this bloke who has this stomach bug that they can't get rid of. It's simply not fair on a bloke, I reckon, especially one who is in pain with his mouth wired shut, to have to go to that extent to protect my mates. These people still owe me big time, I reckon.

And I'm sure Jock didn't fall for it — actually, come to think of it, for him it was probably one of those situations of 'I really don't want to know' — but he played along and wrapped up the visit and left. And then ABD returned to his La-Z-Boy chair and the love of the nurses, to get some much-needed rest. Thankfully, when I woke up at 6 o'clock the next morning ABC and ABD were nowhere to be seen — snuck out under cover of darkness.

All I'm really trying to get across here is that if you ever have a mate or a family member who has broken his jaw, be nice to him. Don't make cruel jokes at his expense; don't think it's funny to get pissed and cause havoc in his hospital room; and don't think it's funny that he has to eat nothing but soup for the next six weeks.

Because if you do, you better be aware that when that man has got his mouth wired shut, he can't brush his teeth. And no matter how much mouthwash he goes through, his breath will still be rancid. So if you give this man crap, all he has to do is breathe on you and you'll be the one who is sorriest.

Just a little piece of advice for you to keep in mind, that's all.

HOW LINEOUTS WORK — OR DON'T WORK, DEPENDING ON WHAT WENT WRONG AT THE TIME

When a lineout goes wrong, it goes wrong in such an obvious way that even the thickest of rugby pundits can see that it went wrong. We threw the ball in; they ended up with it. Not exactly much of what you'd call a 'grey area' with that. It's a very simple equation, so therefore the answer must be equally simple: blame the hooker, because he's the one who threw the bloody ball in.

Oh, if only it were as simple as that — that every lineout the All Blacks have ever lost came down to Andrew Hore or Keven Mealamu or Anton Oliver or even Fitzy and so on, back through time. That'd be nice and easy, wouldn't it? It'd also be crap, but at least none of the blame would come my way.

169

Look, the lineout works like this: an equal or differing number of players from opposing teams line up in two lines that may or may not be (a) straight, (b) in the right place and/or (c) the legally required distance apart. As the hooker prepares to throw the ball in, these players may or may not start moving around in ways that may or may not be part of the plan that the team throwing the ball in is hoping to implement. As they are moving or not moving, the players from both sides may or may not be breaking the laws of the game, and the referee may or may not decide to call a halt to proceedings to inform them that he may or may not penalise them if they don't get their shit together. While all this is going on, the hooker, who has probably just scraped himself off the bottom of a ruck after having his head mashed into the turf, must also hear the lineout call (above the noise of the South African crowd baying for his blood, for example) and remember said call (which may or may not involve a series of letters, numbers, words and/or names of various fruits and which the lineout caller and the lineout jumpers may or may not have remembered correctly).

How could anything possibly go wrong?

I think the best way for someone who doesn't regularly play in the forwards to imagine what a shambles each and every lineout potentially is, and what a hell of a job the hooker in a rugby team has, is by picturing it as something along the lines of:

It's like playing darts, on a dartboard down at the pub or in your garage. Except that here the dartboard is almost 4 metres in the air and is moving around. But not only is it moving around because there are a couple of blokes holding up the guy holding

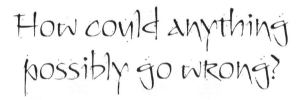

Paul O'Connell and me attempting the rarely seen reverse aerial high five.

171

the dartboard, it's not even the dartboard you're meant to hit. That dartboard is the dartboard *behind* that dartboard, which is also moving around, 4 metres in the air. Add to this the fact that the other team is trying to guess which one of these dartboards you're aiming for, so they can get their dartboard in the way. Then realise that you have to hit the centre of the dartboard because if you hit it to one side the referees will probably ping you for not throwing the dart straight.

Look, don't automatically blame the hookers, alright? Blame me if you need to blame someone, even if I'm not actually playing, because I can live with it.

Good, glad we finally got that sorted out.

Just by looking at it you can tell this is one that went wrong.

ON MATTERS
CONCERNING OUR ANTHEM AND THE SINGING (OR NOT) THEREOF

Every now and then — usually when the All Blacks are going through a rough patch (as happens from time to time with all professional sports teams) — someone in the media will burst into print about how the ABs don't exactly belt into the singing of 'God Defend New Zealand' before test matches. It's always good when the media focus on the important stuff.

Personally, I love singing the anthem and I try to belt it out as loud as humanly possible. There are a bunch of us who share this view and we tend to stand together. It's undoubtedly not very tuneful but it's from the heart and that's all that counts, I reckon. And, yeah, I'll confess that I'm still not completely fluent on the Maori version — on occasions I can get the odd hiccup here and there — but I'm

See? Singing. You happy now?

out there giving it a crack, which I think is important. I'm not a real superstitious person but, for me, when the music's over and I feel I've had a good bellow at it, made a bit of noise, then I'm going to have a good game. But then I'm a noisy bugger at the best of times.

And then there are the guys who don't really get off on singing, who like to use the time to focus on what they've got ahead of them. And that's good too; that's what they need to do. But what people need to know — especially the people in the media who stir up this stuff — is that when the camera tracks past them, as it goes down the line, just because they're not singing doesn't mean they're not giving the anthem the respect it deserves. They're just not singing, that's all; where's the problem with that?

I'm going to go out on a limb now — and I'll probably end up getting in trouble for it, but what the hell — and say that the New Zealand national anthem isn't exactly the most stirring national anthem on the planet.

When you've stood on the turf at the Millennium Stadium in Cardiff, listening to 70,000 Welshmen belting out 'Land of My Fathers', just getting louder and louder and louder; now *that* is a national anthem. That is simply an awesome experience.

175

And then there are teams, like France and Argentina and Italy, who throw themselves into their national anthem with a passion, because that's their thing; that's where they get that outpouring of passion they need before a game. We have the haka for that. That's our time for getting how passionate we feel about representing our country out onto the stage. Different strokes for different folks.

So can we please put this one to bed once and for all? Some people, like me, like to sing; some people don't. There is no right or wrong, either way. If you want TV pictures of people giving it heaps and singing up a storm, point the camera at them and leave the other blokes to their thoughts.

It's not that hard, really.

BEST REFEREE EVER?

Me.

WORST REFEREEING PERFORMANCE EVER?

Do I need to state the obvious?

ALI'S SERIOUSLY WELL-RESEARCHED TRAVEL TIPS

As a professional athlete, I travel many miles by air over the course of a year. Here are a few tips I've picked up along the way:

🐾 Always put your shoes in your suitcase last. Never put them at the bottom of your suitcase because the weight of everything on top of them can crush the heels of your shoes, bend them in a bit, so that the next time you wear them they will give you blisters.

🐾 For long-distance flights, always wear your skins or those stocking things that help prevent deep vein thrombosis. But, even more important, always wash them before the next flight. Not to do so is a cardinal sin; one that is not appreciated by your fellow travelling team-mates.

In transit — and hoping like hell Andrew Hore doesn't mistake me for a seal.

- The night before a long-distance flight go out and stay up as long as humanly possible. I'm not talking go out and get drunk going out; I'm talking about muscling up and staying awake, so that when you get to your flight the next day, you will crash out and sleep for most of it. Don't try to stay up by sitting on the couch and watching TV because that doesn't work and all you will do is fall asleep on the couch, which defeats the point. Go out out; be around people who will help keep you awake until it's time to go to the airport. You must arrive at the airport a completely sleep-deprived wreck if this is going to work.

- Travelling business class really helps with everything — especially if you're 2 metres tall. The upgrade rules.

When going through customs try to get in the queue in front of dodgy-looking people like Ma'a Nonu otherwise you will probably be there for ages.

- If you want a nice quiet flight and you don't mind having bugger-all elbow room, sit next to a prop. Yeah, he'll stink, but if you've stayed up late enough the night before you'll crash out pretty soon anyway so you won't notice so much.

Ah, the joy of travel.

🐾 If, on the other hand, you're after plenty of elbow room and you
don't mind someone yapping in your ear the whole journey, then
sit next to a halfback. Again, if you've stayed up late enough the
night before you'll crash out. It won't stop him talking, but you
won't be able to hear it so it works out fine for all concerned.

🐾 Whatever you do, avoid the flight from Rustenburg to
Johannesburg. It's only an hour or so but at that altitude the
altitude sickness can play havoc with a man. Or so I'm told.

Happy travelling and remember that travelling is just dead time;
it doesn't exist in the real world so don't worry about it too much.
Oh, and don't worry about your bags either — they'll either turn
up or they won't.

SOMETIMES COOL THINGS JUST HAPPEN

I guess there's this idea that when you're an All Black the fitness work is all about trainers and training programmes and flash gyms and that sort of stuff, but the reality is still that the bulk of it is you, pounding the streets or running up and down hills or, in the case of this story, going to the nearest park and doing stuff there.

Dan Carter, Jimmy Cowan and I were down at Cox's Bay Reserve, doing intervals. We'd been there a while when this bloke, who'd been watching us from his house, came down and joined in. He had his old rugby shorts on and all the gear, and he just got stuck in with us.

He was Bryan Williams, one of the greatest All Black wingers ever. For some reason that little moment has stuck with me — one of the coolest players from the past, joining in with us. I'd like to think we inspired him to great heights that day, like he did to us back then.

THE RULES OF ENGAGEMENT

I don't think anyone in the world, apart from Richie McCaw and Daniel Braid, knows the exact laws of rugby. Not the players, not the referees, not the spectators, and certainly not me. Just Richie and Daniel, as far as I can tell.

Mind you, I played soccer for years before I switched to rugby and I've just twigged to the offside law in soccer, 10 years after I stopped playing. Apparently, in soccer, you have to have one of the defending guys, plus the goalkeeper, between you and their goal when one of your players passes you the ball if you're in the opponent's half. Go figure.

How this works if their goalkeeper is like I was and he's up the other end of the field chasing some guy who stood on his nuts is

Jonathan Kaplan explains the finer points of the law to me and Tana. Buggered if I know what that thing is in his hand. Never seen one of them before.

183

anyone's guess. I'm not very good with understanding laws, is what I'm really saying here.

This isn't to say that there aren't laws in rugby. There are plenty of them and there are even people who have studied them and can dish them out on the field: and they're called referees. So maybe all the grey areas that keep springing up aren't so much the laws themselves, but the interpretation of the laws.

Take a scrum, for example. You have three front-rowers on each side, plus a referee, so that's immediately seven people who have an opinion on the laws right there.

Me, I'm just head down and pushing so I don't have an opinion on anything right at that moment — which is probably a good thing.

Anyway, there are these seven people all with an opinion on the laws as regarding the scrum. And six of these people think they are all doing exactly the right thing which means that if the seventh person blows his whistle and awards a penalty, there are at least three of the people who are totally mystified as to why the penalty has been awarded and one of them, the bloke who got singled out for breaking the laws, is totally pissed off because he was doing everything according to the book, so why the hell is he getting picked on?

It all gets a bit confusing out there — and not just for the front-rowers either. In the end, I suppose, you'd argue that the only opinion that matters is that of the bloke with the whistle in his

'Mate, we all know what we're doing — but do you?'

hand, but sometimes they just add to the confusion. They don't mean to; they just do. Like you'll get a referee coming to talk to the coaches before a game, to let them know what they'll be watching for in particular during a game; and then the first incident during the game will be something completely different and suddenly it seems like that's all they're looking out for.

I have a lot of sympathy for referees because it's a bloody hard job. Thirty guys on the paddock at most times in the game, all competing for one ball, all thinking they're doing the right thing and all of them operating under the one true law of any sport: it's only cheating if you get caught. How hard must that be for one bloke?

This is why I often feel I need to give referees the benefit of my advice and experience while I'm on the field. I like to express this in terms of a beer-gained/beer-lost rating of individual decisions. A good decision equals an 'I'll buy you a beer after the game for that, mate' call; while a bad decision means a 'Sorry mate, you know that beer I was going to buy you? Not after that one, mate'. It's a pretty simple rating system that most referees seem not to mind.

I do think, however, that referees — whether they admit it or not — do dish out penalties on an 'I've penalised the other guys a couple of times, so now it's their turn' basis.

You can't really blame them for this when you consider a lot of the calls they make are pretty much 50/50 calls anyway, so to ping one team all the time doesn't really sit right. At the end of a game I reckon if a referee can look at the penalty count and it's about even, then he'll consider he's had a good game; that he's been neutral. And he'll hope the people who judge what he does will look on that the same way so that he can get to referee more games. In the end it's all just human nature and what people want out of a good, clean game, isn't it?

And it can't be easy for referees either, when they keep changing the laws. More confusion all round. I know for players it's a case of learning the new laws and then figuring out the best way to take advantage of the new laws or, if you're not so quick off the mark, to figure out how to combat the team who figured it out before you. Then, just when everyone's got the new law sorted and we're getting back to the game without either team having much of an advantage, they go and change the law again, so everyone's back to square one. Why do they need to keep changing the laws? They don't keep changing the laws in soccer (as far as I can understand the laws of soccer) and that seems to be doing alright as a global sport.

I must read this book one day.

I guess, at the end of the day, what all these law changes are attempting to do is simplify the game, to make it more of an honest, open contest.

I have no problem with that as an idea but if I could add my voice to the mix, can we please bring back rucking?

Rucking — and not in the malicious way of someone walking all over someone's head — simplified the game like you wouldn't believe. Some guy gets caught in the first five minutes where he

'Me? Cheat? You're kidding, right?'

shouldn't be, doing something he shouldn't, trying to slow the ball down, and he gets well and truly rucked? Each time that man gets the opportunity to do the same thing through the rest of the game, he's going to think twice before going there again. Of course, the other side of rucking was wearing the stripes as a badge of honour, so now there's no real grading system in the showers, apart from the obvious.

So many laws, so many interpretations, so many changes, so much confusion. Probably the best way of sorting things out is to get Richie and Daniel to sit everyone down — players, referees, coaches — and explain the way it should be. Yeah, I reckon that could work.

THE ROCK MONSTERS
OF FACIAL HAIR

There's a thing that happens from time to time with rugby teams, particularly in Super 14 franchises, where the facial hair of everyone in the team starts developing a life of its own. Strange and potentially disturbing things start happening in the whisker department, things that normally shouldn't happen among a group of allegedly grown men, as everyone starts sprouting for all they're worth.

Often this is put down to superstition; that a team gets on a winning streak and a pact is made not to touch the facial hair, lest the streak come to an end. While this may be the case in certain franchises (certainly there are times when the Hurricanes need all the help they can get) superstition has never played a part in any of the growth spurts I've been involved in.

Some might think it's about intimidating the opposition; that if you're standing across the lineout from some guy who looks like he's just come out of the jungle and he's got a gorse bush growing out of his face, that you are somehow intimidated by all that hair in a 'What the hell's this monster going to do?' kind of way. But it's not really about that either — except when it comes to the stench that truly hairy men give off.

No, these outpourings of facial growth have, in my experience, generally all been about good old-fashioned team building through money changing hands. They are competitions, with (at times) not insubstantial piles of loot at stake when the winner is judged.

> At first, with the Blues, it was simply about who could grow the most facial hair. Everyone would put in a hundred bucks and away you'd go.

But then the players in the team started getting younger and younger so the rules of the competition changed, to be less about quantity and more about style — what fitted the face best; points for design; and who ended up looking most like a porn star, that sort of thing.

With the Crusaders, it got taken a step further in that everyone had to draw a style of facial hair out of a hat and grow that. There was all sorts of stupid shit in that hat — the full Mexican job, the big chops, that one where you can only grow hair under your chin

Dear God, what kind of creature is this?

191

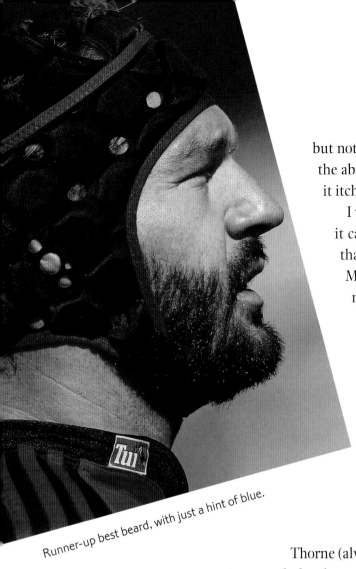

Runner-up best beard, with just a hint of blue.

but not on your face — that one would be the absolute worst, because that's where it itches most.

I was lucky, I got the full beard. And it came out alright except for the fact that there was a fair whack of the old M'orange creeping into it, which made the whole thing look kinda half-arsed. I mean, I'd put the full effort into it, but it just wasn't dark enough. So I got some stuff to dye it darker. It was meant to come out black, but it ended up with this metallic blue shimmer through it (s'pose that's kind of appropriate for an Aucklander down in Canterbury). I ended up coming second to Reuben Thorne (always a good one for the facial hair), not so much for the growth, I reckon, but for my effort and dedication to the cause, I think.

So that's the story behind the facial hair nonsense that grips teams from time to time. It's all good clean fun, except for the bit where it itches like hell, and about the only other thing you need to know about it is never to get involved in any competition like this that also involves Andrew Hore or Jason Eaton 'cause they are rock monsters who go right off the Richter scale in the hair department.

THE TRUTH ABOUT 7
OF THE GREATEST TEST TRIES

TRY #1

VERSUS: Wales
AT: Telstra Stadium
                  Sydney (World Cup, 2 November 2003)
FINAL SCORE: New Zealand 53 Wales 37

THE OFFICIAL VERSION:

Fourth try of the first half; a beauty as 2.02-m Ali Williams
out-jumps 1.70-m Welsh wing Shane Williams to field a Carlos
Spencer cross-kick to secure the bonus point.

MR WILLIAMS' RECOLLECTION OF EVENTS:

Soared, with grace and finesse, above a powerful and tricky
opponent to score the try that would break Welsh resistance.

TRY # 2

VERSUS: Fiji

AT: North Harbour Stadium
Auckland (10 June 2005)

FINAL SCORE: New Zealand 91 Fiji 0

THE OFFICIAL VERSION:

At some stage in the second half, with New Zealand already 50+ points up, Ali Williams waltzed under the bar.

MR WILLIAMS' RECOLLECTION OF EVENTS:

Yeah, okay, the bang-on easiest try anyone will ever score. Next.

Opposite: Try 1. See? Grace *and* finesse.

Above: Try 2. Not exactly the most difficult try ever scored.

TRY # 3

VERSUS: British & Irish Lions

AT: Jade Stadium
Christchurch (25 June 2005)

FINAL SCORE: New Zealand 21 British & Irish Lions 3

THE OFFICIAL VERSION:

On the back of a Lions lineout implosion, Williams snatched a
Lions throw 5 m out and found textbook body position on his way
to the tryline to put the All Blacks 11–0 up.

MR WILLIAMS' RECOLLECTION OF EVENTS:

Carried 15 men on my back, over the line with me, to score.

Try 3. Honest, there were 15 men on my back. You just can't quite see
them all in this photo.

TRY # 4

VERSUS: British & Irish Lions
AT: Eden Park
Auckland (9 July 2005)
FINAL SCORE: New Zealand 38 British & Irish Lions 19

THE OFFICIAL VERSION:

A soft try as Lions halfback failed to control a Luke McAlister grubber into the Lions in-goal and lock Ali Williams pounced.

MR WILLIAMS' RECOLLECTION OF EVENTS:

Used speed, agility, grace and stealth to pounce like a cat on a mouse.

Try 4. Pounced like a black panther, mate.

TRY #5

VERSUS: Portugal

AT: Stade de Gerland

Lyon (World Cup, 15 September 2007)

FINAL SCORE: New Zealand 108 Portugal 13

THE OFFICIAL VERSION:

An Isaia Toeava break provided quick rucked ball for Brendon Leonard to fire a sweeping pass to a midfield assembly of All Blacks and it was lock Ali Williams who grasped it to score.

MR WILLIAMS' RECOLLECTION OF EVENTS:

The pass wasn't meant for me but I couldn't resist.

Try 5. The Portuguese fall to the power of the rat's tail.

TRY #6

VERSUS: Scotland

AT: Murrayfield

Edinburgh (World Cup, 23 September 2007)

FINAL SCORE: New Zealand 40 Scotland 0

THE OFFICIAL VERSION:

Williams circled behind a backs move to score in the corner.

MR WILLIAMS' RECOLLECTION OF EVENTS:

Fended off the entire Scottish nation to score in the corner. Lucky I have long arms otherwise would not have made it.

Try 6. Showing the wingers how it's done.

TRY #7

VERSUS: Samoa

AT: Yarrow Stadium
New Plymouth (3 September 2008)

FINAL SCORE: New Zealand 101 Samoa 14

THE OFFICIAL VERSION:

Some scrappy Samoan play gifted the All Blacks more points when Conrad Smith collected, then passed inside to Ma'a Nonu who then passed to lock Ali Williams who scored the All Black's tenth try of the night.

MR WILLIAMS' RECOLLECTION OF EVENTS:

Being the senior player I made Ma'a pass the ball to me.

Try 7. Ma'a Nonu — a man who knows when to pass.

SOME INTERESTING STATS ABOUT ALI WILLIAMS' TEST TRIES

- The All Blacks have never lost a game in which Ali Williams has scored a test try.

- The All Blacks have lost nine games in which Ali Williams has played but *not* scored a test try. In four of those losses, if Ali Williams had scored a test try the All Blacks would have won. In another they would have won as long as the conversion went over.

- In none of the seven games in which Ali Williams has scored a test try has his try made the slightest bit of difference, on the scoreboard, to whether the All Blacks won or lost.

- In the matches in which Ali Williams has scored a test try, the All Blacks have outscored their opponents 452 points to 86. This is an average winning score of 64.57 to 12.85; with an average winning margin of 51.72.

- In three of the seven games in which Ali Williams scored a test try the referee was South African. Ali Williams has yet to score a test try against South Africa. Whether this is suspicious or not is impossible to judge.

- Ali Williams has never scored two test tries on the same ground.

- Ali Williams' two tries at the 2007 Rugby World Cup left him 31st= on the list of Top Try-scorers for the tournament, along with such players as Kosuke Endo (Japan), Takudzwa Ngwenya (USA), Sukanaivalu Hufanga (Tonga) and Kameli Ratuvou (Fiji).

201

THOU SHALT KILL

There's no easy way of saying this, so I'll just come straight out and say it: there is nothing wrong with a man arming himself, then going out and killing things. Obviously, there are things you shouldn't kill and ways you shouldn't kill them, but in terms of hunting and fishing, two of my favourite things in the entire world, all we're doing is following our evolutionary path, right?

Sure, these days we're better armed than when we came down from the trees in search of food, all those heaps of years ago, but the idea is still the same.

'Man need to go hunt now.' That's a phrase that still rings as true today as it did back when we first learned to say 'Man need to go hunt now'. Okay, yeah, nowadays it's less about bringing food back to the cave and more about talking shit as you fish and throwing back all the small stuff until you catch the fish that gives you bragging rights over your mates, but the principle is the same. Plus you get to sink more quiet ones if you're floating round fishing, than back when early bloke was running round chasing woolly mammoths and trying not to get eaten by the sabre-toothed tigers.

Now, there are a few points I feel I need to make about this whole hunting/shooting/fishing lark, before anyone gets on my case about being a barbarian. These are:

Going out to catch/shoot stuff gives blokes a chance to use a part of the brain they very rarely get in touch with. Often the only time a male will be any good at planning is when it comes to organising a hunting or fishing trip.

Normally, men just go and do things, without much thought about any actual organisation.

The hunter has entered the forest.

But if you get a bunch of guys planning an expedition that involves food, a boat, guns, ammo, bait, rods, beer, somewhere to sleep, transport in and out and all that palaver, suddenly you've got some excited guys. It's the thrill of the hunt, literally.

It's a healthy way for men to share their feelings. For it is a widely known fact that men cannot talk to each other and share their thoughts on the state of the world, unless they are standing alongside each other, sharing in some common activity and not looking at each other. This is because guys need an out clause in any conversation, in case things start getting a bit personal, a bit dodgy; like the weather or why the fish aren't biting and so forth. Thus doing this stuff while out fishing is much healthier than doing it while you're sitting on the couch playing video games.

Animals everywhere fear this man.

It's a great chance for men to show they can care about each other. Like the story of how my mates dug an extra little trench at the end of the mai-mai just for me, when I went out duck shooting one time, just so I wouldn't have to crouch down. That's real thoughtful stuff. The same story goes for how when I had my broken jaw and couldn't eat meat and I was out shooting — they made sure the barbecue was set up as far away from me as possible. That's the sort of manly consideration that is too rare in this world these days.

It's not just the random killing of an animal that comes along. I personally wouldn't want to hunt the Big Five (lion, African elephant, Cape buffalo, leopard and black rhino) just to fulfil some

Portrait of a man gathering the kai from the moana.

macho fantasy. Ducks and rabbits, on the other hand, I would blast away merrily at them. Every hunter draws their own line in the sand about what they will or will not take a pot at. With Andrew Hore, for example, his line is somewhere just above seals.

As well as shooting animals, you get to bond with them as well. I have been known to wade into the lake, with the dogs, to pick up the fallen ducks.

This gives both the dogs and the boys a bit of a laugh and can do wonders for the spirits of man and beast (except for the ducks, obviously).

Sometimes the animals win. Like the time I was shooting in a swan cull when a swan fell out of the sky and took out this bloke in the line just along from me. This dead swan, which is a lot of bird, falling from a great height, just absolutely smoked this poor guy; so just because we've got all the technology, doesn't mean it is all one-way traffic.

And whether you do or don't catch anything isn't really the point. It's the thrill of trying that is the important thing and also locking down quality time to talk shit with your mates.

Yeah, the talking shit thing is very significant in all this. Just in case you hadn't guessed.

A rare photo of me playing for the Blues in 2007.

IT TAKES TWO TO TANGO

You ever have one of those years you wish you could just take back? That was 2007 for me. The broken jaw and the bloody French in the quarter-final; that's more than enough for any man; except then I have to throw into the mix the whole 'getting sent home from South Africa' debacle. 2007: what a top year that was, professionally and personally.

Just to fill in the details, the whole sorry shambles played out something like this: we, the Blues, played our last round-robin game of the 2007 Super 14 in Perth, on Friday. After beating the Force we had a bit of a team night out before we had to fly to Sydney on Saturday, to wait to see if we'd be flying out to South Africa for the semi-final. Sunday morning we flew out to Jo'burg, to make our way to Durban to play the Sharks. Or not. Because when we got to Jo'burg, management got the players to say to me, at the airport, 'Mate, we're sending you home' — because I'd apparently breached all these team protocols.

What is breaching protocol, anyway? Apparently, if you believe what you read in the paper, I breached one protocol by abusing a waitress. Funny thing is, the way I remember it, I ordered the Chef's Special at dinner (it was chicken, actually) and at the end of the meal she asked me how it was. And me, being one of those guys who calls it like he sees it when it comes to eating out, said, 'Well, let's just say the Chef's Special wasn't that special.' I wasn't being rude, I was just telling the truth, but by the time it got filtered through management, apparently I 'caused embarrassment to the worker' and to my team-mates.

Is going out for a few beers in Perth, to celebrate my birthday, on a Tuesday night, with my mates and several management members (as well as several members of the American Navy as it turned out, but that's another story), abusing team protocols?

Okay, I was a bit late in — three, four, five o'clock late, I wasn't really counting — and I'd be the first one to put my hand up and say that's not entirely the most professional thing to do.

But I wouldn't call it something worthy of getting all the way to South Africa, only to be told to turn around and piss off back home.

People keep asking me what the true story was behind all this — what did I do? Were there full blown arguments going on between

210

me and the coach and the rest of the management and team? The answer is no; the answer is that I got sent home because things just kept building and building, without it ever getting sorted out.

In the end, this is the story about a player and a coach who really didn't get on and how that situation — where both parties don't really have respect for each other — can get totally out of control. When you're in that situation, it can turn to custard real quick, let me tell you.

I think maybe some of the fallout between me and the coach started way back, when he first came into the team as a technical advisor and high-performance manager.

There was one 'incident', if you want to call it that, but it's stuck with me this long so it must have meant something. It was at an end-of-season booze-up and we're playing this game where if you go up to someone and give them a tap on the arm, they have to down their beer; and if someone gives you the tap, you have to do the same.

Now, just to set the scene, at these sorts of sessions, in my experience anyway, the players generally stick together, and the coaches and management stick together. It's not a hard and fast rule; it's generally just the way these things pan out. In some cases there are coaching and management bods you're happy mingling with, like Peter Sloane, who was the coach before David Nucifora turned up. I got on well with him.

Anyway, we're all at this drinking session, I think it was after the 2005 Super 12 season, and I decided it was about time to bridge the gap, so I went up to Nucifora, gave him the tap, said, 'Chop your beer, mate.' I don't think it went down too well. In fact, I think he looked at me like 'Who the hell is this idiot?' You know, maybe I'm over-reading that moment, but like I say, it stuck in my mind, so maybe it was a sign of things to come.

Some coaches I can really get on with. Steve Hansen, for example, I wind up all the time — and he gives back as good as he gets. That's pretty much the level of me and Shag getting on.

With me and Nucifora, it was fair to say we never ever got on that same wavelength.

So fast forward to 2007 and it's a World Cup year and the year of the whole conditioning programme that meant 22 All Blacks, me included, missed the first seven rounds of the Super 14. I don't want to get into all the politics that goes on (and will always go on) between the All Blacks management and the Super 14 franchises,

Peter Sloane and David Nucifora. I think it's fair to say I got on better with one of these blokes than the other.

but I think it's fair to say that back in 2007 there wasn't a lot of what you'd call agreement between the All Black management and the Blues management, particularly the coach, about how to handle this conditioning programme. The All Black coaches, they gave us what we needed to do, set up the programme, then let us go and do our stuff. We knew what we had to achieve and what we needed to do to get there.

But the Blues wanted it run totally differently. They said we had to train at the same time they trained. They said we had to wear Blues training gear while we were training. We had to be at every game, in our number ones dress uniform, to show we were still part of the team. It just went on and on, until I got up — as the lippiest of the bunch away being conditioned — and I pointed out, in no uncertain terms, that part of the whole conditioning thing was not only to get us physically right for the World Cup, but to get us mentally away from rugby so we'd arrive there fresh. So having all this other stuff loaded on top of you, it really wasn't helping matters.

There were two very different environments: the Blues, and the guys doing the conditioning programme. Now some of the conditioning guys were happy to go along with the Blues protocols (there's that word again) and I am cool with that — it definitely wasn't an 'us and them' situation in that sense, on a team level. But if I'm meant to go to every Blues home game, when I'm not playing, I'd quite like to go with my old man, rather than be a non-playing member of the squad for that night. I didn't — and still don't — see what's so wrong with that.

It's not like the guys on the conditioning programme were slacking around. We were training bloody hard. But we were doing our own thing, which didn't mesh well with certain people's thinking about how things should be done. And because I'm me and I can't help myself, I basically became the voice for the guys doing the conditioning: asking the really basic questions about why we were being asked to do things in a certain way when the ABs from the other franchises weren't being asked to do these things.

And when what I started getting in return was 'Look at this guy, he's just in it for his own reasons. He wants to be an All Black; he doesn't really care about the Blues,' that's when it really started to hurt, because that was never ever the case.

The first day back in the team after conditioning, we were doing this thing called pure assessment, where basically you stand up in front of the whole team and say the stuff you think you're doing good at; the stuff you think you're not good at; and the stuff you need help with. Then everyone does the same back to you; giving you their honest assessment about who you are and how you're fitting in. So I got up and said my piece and then the other players got up and said what they wanted to say, which was basically all good.

And then management got up and laid into me. First day back and they came at me swinging. At first I was stunned — 'What the hell is going on here?' In the end I was devastated.

After the conditioning we were expected to rejoin our teams, halfway through the Super 14 season. I knew, we all knew, you couldn't expect to walk back into the team, especially if the guys who have been playing thus far have been doing the business. I knew I had to fight my way back into the team, but how can you fight, how can you prove what you've got, when you can't get on the field?

As a player, any player, not just me or any of the other guys coming back into the squad after the conditioning programme, you can only respect the coach if he delivers on what he says to you. If he says to you, on Thursday, when you know you're going to be warming the bench, 'We'll give you 20 minutes at the end,' and then Saturday night you're still sitting there with five minutes to go thinking 'What the hell?', then that doesn't exactly gain you much respect, in my book. If you say, 'We'll read how the game's going before putting you on, Ali,' then that's fine, I can work with that.

Yeah, I'll be pissed off to be on the sidelines, but at least I'm not sitting on my arse waiting for something I've been promised, which then never happens.

In the end I got sick of it and then, by the time we went on the South Africa road-trip and then back to Perth, I'd pretty much started doing my own thing. I didn't feel I was getting the respect, and I guess I wasn't giving a hell of a lot back. It takes two to tango, right? And, if I let myself down anywhere, it was in getting myself

'Okay, how am I going to talk my way out of this one?'

into this headspace. I desperately wanted to play, but I wasn't dealing with all the other shit going on around me.

The worst thing about all this, and what went on in South Africa, was how the other players were used by management to isolate me and then to tell me to bugger off back to New Zealand. That was hard for them — they were the middle men in a fight that shouldn't have been theirs. These were my mates, guys I really respect, and they were backed into a corner.

So when they came to me to tell me what was going on, I didn't argue. I said, 'Yeah, okay, I'll go home.' I will confess I wasn't as polite when the coach came up to me and told me I knew the reasons why this was happening. And by the time management were trying to tell me how this was going to work, I was well over everything. Bugger you, I'll book myself into a hotel and send you an invoice, was about the extent of the dialogue here. Which is exactly what I did.

People told me, when I got back to New Zealand, that I had a case for unfair dismissal under employment law and all that, but I couldn't be bothered with all that stuff. In the end it was all about two guys who really didn't see eye to eye on just about everything. And then the All Black coaches were awesome about the whole bloody mess, which took a whole lot of stress out of it.

And then I solved everything by moving down to Christchurch — and having a thoroughly enjoyable time, which is most definitely the end of this particular story.

HOW TO PASS THE TIME IN CHRISTCHURCH

So back in 2007 I fell out with certain people up in Auckland and the upshot was I took off down to Christchurch to play my rugby in 2008. Of course, being an Aucklander all my life, then heading down there, you expect to cop a bit of the Jaffa horse-shit that follows Aucklanders around. But it was all good. Almost everyone was very polite and it was nice being out of the spotlight a bit, with a new team and a new coach.

I was staying, for most of the week, with Richie, at his place in a part of Christchurch that is basically a retirement village. Richie, to put it politely, is a freak. The way he plays; the abuse he puts his body through; freakish. And his self-discipline is remarkable. So he was obviously a real good guy for me to be around for a while, especially after the nightmares of the previous season.

When you're living in Christchurch, there's not exactly a lot to do. It's really nice and chilled out, which I like. So it forces you to find things to do other than eating beef schnitzel which is what Richie cooks all the time. I got my dive ticket, which was good. There were evenings where Dan and I would sit round, in our respective super-hero outfits, playing video games, but doesn't everyone do shit like that? Oh, and I broke up a fight and ended up on TV for it, looking like a real hero for once in my life.

To be completely honest, however, it wasn't actually as heroic as it got painted on the news. Ross Filipo and I were having a quiet stroll around town, of an evening, when we saw a scuffle break out. So we stopped to watch, as you do. But as we're standing there, trying to pick who is going to win, things started getting ugly as all these guys started picking on one guy.

'This isn't right, mate. He's going to get bashed. We should stop this.'

So there's a bit of a debate between me and Floss about the best way to stop this thing — and whether, if we wade in, they'll all turn on us and clean our clocks instead.

'Okay, buddy,' I say, eventually. 'I have an idea.'

And with that I began bellowing, like some demented stag, and started walking towards them. And I'm bellowing away like a mad thing, and they all stop fighting and start looking at me like 'Who is this dickhead?' So by the time I got amongst it, with Floss behind me, the fighting had basically broken up already. No heroics, just giving these guys something else to get fixated on, i.e. 'Who is this great big moron and why is he bellowing at us like some demented stag?'

Of course, about two seconds later, when they realise who we are, the phones are out and it's all 'Oh my girlfriend, you know, she really likes you — can I get a photo?' So there's peace in Christchurch and Spiderman and the Phantom have saved the day, in their own special way.

Another thing that happened in Christchurch, that year, was that Richie and I bought remote-control aeroplanes and learnt to fly them, because what else do you do in Christchurch, if you're not into gardening?

Richie's plane was bigger than my plane and easier to fly. Being a bit of a show-boat I got this little nippy number, figuring I'd be doing all these aerobatics in no time. Of course, his was the plane that ended up staying all nice and pristine, while mine was the one that kept crashing; not that this was entirely all down to me trying to be a big show-off, I have to say.

We'd go down to the park near Richie's place to fly, and we were down there this one time when Richie's plane stopped working, so being a generous bloke I handed over the controls of my plane to Richie: 'Go on, have a go with this one, mate.' And he's cruising it around the skies of Christchurch, doing very well, for a while; up to the point where I figured he's being a bit conservative with it.

'Give it the loop-de-loop!' says the flashy Aucklander to the sensible Cantabrian.

So he does. And he loop-de-loops it straight into a bloody tree.

So there's my plane, stuck up this bloody great tree. The motor's still working, but it isn't going anywhere in a hurry, no matter what we try. And there are these two kids down there, kicking a rugby ball around, and they come over to see why the All Black captain and his lanky offsider are staring up at a tree.

'Your plane's stuck up the tree.'

Gee, no kidding.

'We'll get it out for you.'

So here are these two kids, trying to climb up the tree to get my plane (which, I remind you, Richie crashed into the tree, not me) out of the tree. And we're all kicking the rugby ball up into the tree, trying to knock it out. It's all a bit of a shambles really. But, eventually, the plane came out of the tree — and that was a shambles too.

And that was the end of my plane — after, just to make this point crystal clear one last time, Richie McCaw, the All Black captain, crashed it into a tree.

But Richie got pretty flash at flying his plane, up to the point where he could use his driveway as a landing strip. He'd get the plane taking off, then fly it around the retirement village for a bit, then bring it back in. This is until the day he misjudged everything and flew it straight into his neighbour's house.

Richie: 'Go on, you go get it.'

Ali: 'Me? Why do I have to get it? You crashed it!'

So, of course, eventually I go and retrieve the plane from the oldies' backyard because, of course, I'm a good boy who always does what he's told — especially in Christchurch where everyone is more polite.

Eventually, we forgot about the planes and bought a miniature helicopter. We initially started flying round Richie's lounge. Then we stepped up to flying it round Richie's tiny backyard. Then we took it out into the wide open spaces, because we figured we'd got the hang of it. We hadn't. We crashed it and the damned thing hasn't worked since.

And that's how you pass the time for a year in Christchurch.

Oh yeah, and we won the Super 14, which is also not a bad way to pass the time in Christchurch.

THE POWER OF THE JERSEY

On the All Blacks' end-of-year tour, 2008, adidas took some of the boys to Milan, to check out the AC Milan training facility and to meet some of the Milan players. These are people like Clarence Seedorf, Ronaldinho and Kaka (before he got transferred to Real Madrid for somewhere in the stratosphere of $136,000,000, which is an insane amount of money in anyone's world).

In other words, these guys are footballing royalty, and we're a bunch of roosters from this tiny country down the other end of the world (one that Kaka could probably buy now, if he felt like it).

While we were there, because I used to be a goalie when I was a kid, they stuck me in goal and we had a penalty shootout. Holy shit, those guys are good. They made making me look silly look easy. The bloke they stuck in goal was a guy my size, by the name of Zeljko Kalac, an Australian guy who was their reserve keeper until he got axed before the 2009–10 'Serie A' season. He was a really good guy.

Afterwards, after they'd embarrassed me, we did this thing with soccer balls and rugby balls, kicking them into balloons filled with paint, and the paint would go everywhere, on these posters with 'Impossible is Nothing' written on them. But what interested me was how once we'd finished this, it was the Milan boys who were the first to grab the rugby balls and come up to us for autographs. So there's a kid like Alby Mathewson, on his first tour, he's played about 30 minutes on the whole tour, signing this ball for Kaka, who is pretty much the world's best soccer player. And all the Milan boys are yelling out, 'Hey, Kaka! Never thought I'd see the day you asked for an autograph!' It was mind blowing.

Dan and Kaka. One is very rich, the other is famous for his undies.

But that's the power of the jersey; the All Black jersey.

We had a few beers with Kalac after the session and he turned out to be this guy, from a fairly rough background in Australia, who thought it was a bit of a joke that he's taking home a couple of million Euros a year, just to be the back-up keeper. But what he missed most was what the All Blacks have, which is this team mentality that means we stick together.

The power of the jersey, again.

The world this guy was describing was about a bunch of highly paid individuals who turn up to play and to train, then bugger off in their separate directions, in their flash cars. No socialising; not even ringing each other for a yarn. He and Seedorf had tried to get a team mentality going, but it never really worked, I guess because some of these guys are still kids who are so famous they can't go anywhere without getting shit, so they don't go anywhere. That's really sad to me.

The All Blacks and the All Black jersey get talked about a lot in terms of being a 'brand' and, yeah, in terms of being something that advertises New Zealand to the world. It is — and that's all good. But when you're inside the All Black team the jersey has its own special power; the power of a collective, reinforced by all the people who have worn the jersey before us, and all the non-playing millions who support us. I know it has made me a better person and it gives me a reason to want to stay in this country for as long as they'll have me.

Respect the power of the All Black jersey, is all I'm saying. Ask Kaka about it; he's knows what I'm talking about — and he's got Alby Mathewson's autograph to prove it.

ALI'S
ALL BLACKS XV

1. Tony Woodcock —
'because some say he's pretty good'

2. Sean Fitzpatrick —
'because he reckons he never
ever threw a ball in crooked in his
entire career'

3. Carl Hayman —
'because he's so good-looking'

4. Brad Thorn — 'because if I don't
select him I'll get in trouble'

5. Someone who isn't Ali Williams —
'he's unavailable due to injury
anyway'

6. Reuben Thorne —
'for his excellent facial hair'

7. Richie McCaw —
'as a favour, because he's not
that flash really'

8. Xavier Rush —
'in return for teaching me
all my bad habits'

9. Jimmy Cowan —
'because even white
trash deserves a chance'

10. Dan Carter —
'okay, whiz kid, you can play too'

11. Jonah Lomu –
'because he might introduce
me to someone nice'

12. Sam Tuitupou –
'because anyone who can down-
trou Graham Henry then give
him a hug deserves to be in the
starting XV'

13. Tana Umaga –
'because he's The Godfather'

14. Doug Howlett –
'so the others can borrow
his hair gel'

15. Mils Muliaina –
'just don't stand near him
in the bar afterwards'

COACH: My dad

THE OPPOSITION XV

1. Ollie le Roux (South Africa) — 'because someone needs to eat all the pies'

2. Sean Fitzpatrick (New Zealand) — 'to make sure the opposition hooker doesn't cheat'

3. Al Baxter (Australia) — 'so his mum can bake everyone biscuits'

4. Murray Deaker (New Zealand) — 'a chance to put his money where his mouth is'

5. Jay Williams (New Zealand) — 'because every team needs a red-head'

6. Zinzan Brooke (New Zealand) — 'in case they need a drop kick to win'

7. Spiderman (USA) — 'do I need a reason?'

8. Either Sione Lauaki (New Zealand) or The Incredible Hulk (USA) — 'they're pretty much the same thing anyway'

9. Jimmy Cowan (New Zealand) — 'because he needs the game time'

10. Carlos Spencer (New Zealand) — 'to do that stuff that only Carlos can do'

11. Michael Hancock (Australia, rugby league) — 'so that everyone can have a laugh when he does that having a fit on the ground thing he used to do when he got tackled'

12. Jonny Wilkinson (England) — 'in case Zinzan misses with the drop kick'

13. Gareth Thomas (Wales) — 'seems like a good rooster despite missing a few teeth'

14. James Small (South Africa) — 'because every team should have a psycho'

15. Mike Catt (England) — 'so Jonah can have someone to walk over'

COACH:	Martin Johnson
REFEREE:	A. Williams (New Zealand)
ASSISTANT REFEREES:	S. Fitzpatrick, R. McCaw, T. Umaga (all New Zealand)
VENUE:	The Garden of Eden, on a nice sunny Saturday afternoon
AFTER-MATCH VENUE:	My place, for a few quiet ones

OH, AND ONE
LAST THING

I'll pretty much answer to anything, whatever anyone calls me at the time, but just for the record my name is Ali, as in 'dear God, you wouldn't want to meet that in a dark alley' and not Ali, as in 'Muhammad Ali was the greatest heavyweight boxer of all time'.

Just thought we should sort that out, once and for all.

MOST SATISFYING VICTORY?

Still to come.